Praise for INTERPI

"Dr. Skube possesses a unique vision, as she incorporates business, the individual, <u>and</u> the soul. **Interpersonal Edge** *is unique in that it challenges the individual on multiple levels—like an internal mission statement. It's a practical tool to help individuals understand how they can prepare themselves for the business world in a down-to-earth manner. For those individuals and corporations who are looking to hit the snooze button, Dr. Skube's* **Interpersonal Edge** *is a no-nonsense wake-up call to action, responsibility, and ownership. In a world of chocolate,* **Interpersonal Edge** *is New York Super Fudge Chunk."*

— **Walt Freese**, Ben & Jerry's CEO (Chief Euphoria Officer)

"Dr. Skube captures the essence of what drives successful business leadership. She offers sound advice on how understanding the perspective of your customers, employees, and communities can help improve your ability to communicate. She also presents her ideas in a concise format that clearly demonstrates the value of the Interpersonal Edge."

— **J. Michael Pocock**, president and CEO, Polaroid Corporation

"It is unusual for a clinician to be able to write with clarity and insights for a general audience. Daneen Skube is one of those rare talents. Through her column in **The Seattle Times***, individuals and businesses in our community have benefited from her common sense and knowledge for many years. As one of America's last family-owned newspapers, she is a perfect fit with our newspaper—one which fosters relationships and family values internally and which tries to provide similar content for its readers. Dr. Skube has been a valuable asset to the* **Times** *and to the community. Readers will benefit immensely from her new book."*

— **Frank A. Blethen**, publisher, *The Seattle Times*

"The Great Law of the Iroquois Confederacy states: 'In our every deliberation, we must consider the impact of our decisions on the next seven generations.' To actually live this ideal, one needs to live life awake . . . the tools Daneen provides in this book will open your eyes to see seven generations out in every moment."

— **Jeffrey Hollender**, president and corporate responsibility officer, Seventh Generation, Inc.

"A must-read for anyone who wants to become more successful by building strong and productive relationships. Whether you desire to strengthen your relationships with clients, associates, or significant others, Dr. Skube's powerful 'toolkits' are indispensable."

— **Nina Ableman**, vice president, Merrill Lynch

INTERPERSONAL
EDGE

HAY HOUSE TITLES OF RELATED INTEREST

Books

The Body Knows, by Caroline Sutherland

The Breakthrough Experience, by Dr. John F. Demartini

Confidence, by Barbara De Angelis, Ph.D.

Dawn Breslin's Power Book, by Dawn Breslin

Empowering Women, by Louise L. Hay

Five Steps for Overcoming Fear and Self-Doubt,
by Wyatt Webb

Passionate People Produce, by Charles Kovess

10 Secrets for Success and Inner Peace, by Dr. Wayne Dyer

The Three Keys to Self-Empowerment, by Stuart Wilde

Trust Your Vibes at Work, and Let Them Work for You,
by Sonia Choquette

You Can Heal Your Life, by Louise L. Hay

INTERPERSONAL
EDGE

Breakthrough Tools for Talking to Anyone, Anywhere, about Anything

DANEEN SKUBE, Ph.D.

HAY HOUSE, INC.
Carlsbad, California
London • Sydney • Johannesburg
Vancouver • Hong Kong

Published and distributed in the United States by: Hay House, Inc., P.O. Box 5100, Carlsbad, CA 92018-5100 • *Phone:* (760) 431-7695 or (800) 654-5126 • *Fax:* (760) 431-6948 or (800) 650-5115 • www.hayhouse.com • *Published and distributed in Australia by:* Hay House Australia Pty. Ltd., 18/36 Ralph St., Alexandria NSW 2015 • *Phone:* 612-9669-4299 • *Fax:* 612-9669-4144 • www.hayhouse.com.au • *Published and distributed in the United Kingdom by:* Hay House UK, Ltd. • Unit 62, Canalot Studios • 222 Kensal Rd., London W10 5BN • *Phone:* 44-20-8962-1230 • *Fax:* 44-20-8962-1239 • www.hayhouse.co.uk • *Published and distributed in the Republic of South Africa by:* Hay House SA (Pty), Ltd., P.O. Box 990, Witkoppen 2068 • *Phone/Fax:* 27-11-706-6612 • orders@psdprom.co.za • *Distributed in Canada by:* Raincoast • 9050 Shaughnessy St., Vancouver, B.C. V6P 6E5 • *Phone:* (604) 323-7100 • *Fax:* (604) 323-2600

Editorial supervision: Jill Kramer • *Design:* Tricia Breidenthal

Body-scan image: Jared Kopp / *Johari window image:* Reprinted by permission of Mayfield Publishing, The McGraw-Hill Companies, from *Group Processes: An Introduction to Group Dynamics*, Joseph Luft, second edition, 1970

The author of this book does not dispense medical advice or prescribe the use of any technique as a form of treatment for physical, emotional, or medical problems without the advice of a physician, either directly or indirectly. The intent of the author is only to offer information of a general nature to help you in your quest for emotional and spiritual well-being. In the event you use any of the information in this book for yourself, which is your constitutional right, the author and the publisher assume no responsibility for your actions.

Library of Congress Cataloging-in-Publication Data

Skube, Daneen.
  Interpersonal edge : breakthrough tools for talking to anyone, anywhere, about anything / Daneen Skube.
     p. cm.
  ISBN-13: 978-1-4019-0879-9 (hardcover)
  ISBN-10: 1-4019-0879-9 (hardcover)
  ISBN-13: 978-1-4019-0880-5 (tradepaper)
  ISBN-10: 1-4019-0880-2 (tradepaper)
  1. Interpersonal communication. 2. Interpersonal relations. I. Title.
  BF637.C45S585 2006
  158.2--dc22
                          2005027525

Hardcover: ISBN 13: 978-1-4019-0879-9 • ISBN 10: 1-4019-0879-9
Tradepaper: ISBN 13: 978-1-4019-0880-5 • ISBN 10: 1-4019-0880-2

09 08 07 06   4 3 2 1
1st printing, February 2006

Printed in the United States of America

TO ARIANA ANGELICA

CONTENTS

PART II: IMPROVING EFFECTIVENESS WITH OTHERS

PART III: IMPROVING EFFECTIVENESS IN THE WORLD

AUTHOR'S NOTE

The tools in this book are very powerful; however, the strategies will only work when you implement them with consideration for others. If people feel that they're being manipulated, they won't support your agenda, no matter how sophisticated your technique.

This book is not a magical "fix." To get optimal results, you'll need to take on new ways of behaving and change familiar habits that don't support the life you want for yourself.

This book may not resolve every relationship or life issue, but it will clearly assist you in recognizing the situations you can't change, and show you how to make a graceful exit.

Warning: This book is hazardous to your ability to stay lonely, poor, and miserable! If you apply the information herein, you'll undoubtedly improve your relationships, expand support for your business, enhance your opportunities for promotion or advancement, increase your ability to make money, and experience greater peace of mind. Proceed with *haste!*

PREFACE

WHY I WROTE THIS BOOK

When I was a young girl, I remember going to the water fountain after watching a vicious fistfight between two kids on the playground. As I drank, I pondered the scene and wondered why our teachers weren't instructing us in how to get along. I figured that understanding how to do so was more important, or at least on a par with, being taught a foreign language—after all, conflict occurs in *all* languages. Even now, after 27 years as a therapist, executive coach, and communication trainer, I still contemplate this question. As a therapist, I'm a trained listener. I've noticed that even when a group of people speak a common tongue like English, I hear different emotional "dialects" depending on who's speaking and where. Men, women, children, families, the workplace, and the home all seem to require different languages, with much information being lost in the translation.

Telling your beloved, "You hurt my feelings," might generate productive changes in a relationship; telling your co-worker the same thing will probably result in your being labeled a wimp. Similarly, you won't get anywhere telling your kids that they "aren't contributing to the bottom line," although your co-workers will likely get that message.

Up until now, there hasn't been a book that presents a common language that works equally well with your boss, your customers, your employees, your sweetheart, your kids, and your friends. So I wrote this work because for years and years I've been observing the suffering our lack of a common or universal language causes in each of us—and I've been developing the tools to create this language since the aforementioned playground incident. My therapy clients have told me I'm the first therapist they've worked with who ever helped them effectively navigate the workplace jungle, and my corporate clients have told me that I'm the first consultant they've worked with who also improved their personal lives. Readers of my popular syndicated column, "Interpersonal Edge," often write to say that they've successfully used the tool from my latest column.

So with this book, I'm now making this common language available to people all over the world. I want all of you to realize that much of your suffering isn't due to personal inadequacies, but simply to not knowing how to speak this universal language.

Interpersonal Edge will teach you how to "kick butt" in the world—and, at the same time, help you evolve spiritually. It's sort of a Donald Trump-marries-Mother Teresa concept. It may seem an unusual match because spirituality is generally associated with making sacrifices, whereas kicking butt is associated with getting ahead at any cost. The common language this book offers you combines a strategic effectiveness with generosity and kindness. You're about to learn the undiscovered secret that getting what you deeply and truly want is actually good for the world. You'll also find out that your unanswered prayers are opportunities to think bigger, not give up.

I've discovered that with the right tools, most "crappy circumstances" and "sour grapes" can be turned into compost for our gardens and wine for our tables.

Even if you have little or no interest in spirituality, this book will still work for you. To give you an analogy, you don't need to believe in electricity to benefit from a power drill. Whether you believe in a higher power or not, you'll find that the tools within this book will automatically reduce your sense of chaos, improve your effectiveness, and increase your peace of mind.

I dedicated this book to my daughter, but on a larger level, it is geared toward the healthy, energetic kid still intact within each one of us. I find that so many people have forgotten that wide-eyed child they once were who looked out to the future as an endless horizon of amazing possibilities. You are precious, you are worth fighting for, and no matter what your history . . . you can still get what you want!

INTRODUCTION

CREATING A LIFE YOU ABSOLUTELY LOVE!

Once upon a time . . . there was a kid. This kid looked a lot like you, had big dreams, a bigger imagination, and knew that life was an adventure full of magic and discovery. Then the kid grew up, found out that Santa Claus wasn't real, the Tooth Fairy was cheap, and "happily ever after" was never the actual end of the story.

This book is about rediscovering the kid you left behind on carefree sunny days when the air was full of the smell of freshly mown grass and countless possibilities. It's also chock-full of strategies, tools, and a language to bring that kid's dreams back to life—no matter where you are or who you're speaking with.

After working with myriad clients for over a quarter of a century, I've noticed that people not only forget their "creative kid" when they grow up, but they also think they have to constantly change *who they are* in order to adapt to different situations. For example, at work, you might think you have to be a tough competitor—then at home, a loving family member. With the guys, you banter about sports and politics—around women, you need to become sensitive and emotional. But when you have the Interpersonal Edge, you can get off this personality merry-go-round because you won't need to change who you are when you're in different situations or with different people. After reading this book, you'll possess a language that works anywhere, with anyone.

In books and movies, heroes and heroines don't need a special language to create magical results. These protagonists effortlessly attract fiercely loyal supporters. Frodo, the hero in *The Lord of the Rings,* has a group of friends, "the Fellowship of the Ring,"who risk life and limb to support his mission. Harry Potter, of course, has his two devoted buddies, Hermione and Ron. Even Dorothy in *The Wizard of Oz* had the steadfast companionship of the Tin Man, the Cowardly Lion, and the Scarecrow.

One of my clients joked that she wished she had a dramatic sound track in her life just like in the movies. I've noticed that this isn't the only way in which films differ from real life. Few of us have relationships that shower us with the unwavering devotion bestowed upon the fictional and fortunate Frodo, Harry, and Dorothy. Instead, *our* relationships tend to feel more like the biblical story of the Tower of Babel, where nobody speaks the same language—so forget about trying to build any towers to heaven!

This book will remind you of who you really are and what you can really do, giving you a universal language to create what you really want to make happen—no matter whom you're communicating with. I've named the language I teach in this book *Social Sorcery,* because using it will create magic and enchantment in what you probably now perceive as an ordinary life. As you begin using Social Sorcery, you'll become a Social Sorcery apprentice—kind of like a real-life Harry Potter—only you'll be working with words, not wands. When you speak with Social Sorcery, you'll have the Interpersonal Edge to build relationships that support your dreams—dreams that will rival those of Frodo, Harry, and Dorothy. All you'll be missing is the sound track, although you can create your own if you'd like.

Social Sorcery will do for your life what regular exercise does for your body. When you work out, you get "buff." When you use Social Sorcery, you'll get the Interpersonal Edge . . . as you shape up your work and home life.

Many of us would like to have a better life—if we could just figure out how. We all know that if we go to the gym, run, or take exercise classes, we'll improve our fitness level. Even if we just walk once or twice a week, we'll end up in better shape. So, in nearly every chapter, you'll find practical toolkits with examples of how my clients have applied these tools to improve their work and home lives. Just as you'd use gym equipment to get in better physical shape, you can use the toolkits to increase your power and effectiveness in *all* areas of your life. Like exercising, Social Sorcery starts working from the minute you "pick up" the first toolkit in this book and try it out.

No matter what has happened to you in the past, after reading this book you'll have the power to turn your life around. When you have the Interpersonal Edge, you'll even know how to handle situations that frustrate you or don't appear to be going your way—so that you *do* get what you want in the long run.

Many self-help and business books focus on providing formulas to communicate in different situations. But life doesn't occur in predictable formulas. Also, when you're stressed, it's unlikely that you'll remember that clever thing you were supposed to say to your boss, or that other witty thing that sometimes works with your spouse. Instead, Social Sorcery gives you a set of easy-to-use tools and shows you how to tailor them for any situation.

Many spiritual books I've read outline the ultimate goal of humanity as evolving toward love. However, in my own life, I've noticed that the concept of "love" is abstract, confusing, and not easy to implement during difficult moments. When my daughter is whining in the backseat of my car, my husband is grumpy, or I can't get some darn customer-service person to help me, what I find most useful is Social Sorcery, the powerful "language" that unequivocally gets my point across, yet is *kind*. *Interpersonal Edge* will show you how to tackle the *real* problems of work and life head-on.

I roll up my sleeves in every chapter to join you in finding answers to handling your tough boss, demanding clients, annoying in-laws, wild kids, and frustrating spouse. Loving yourself and other people is a marvelous intention that goes nowhere without reliable tools to achieve this worthy goal. So if you've ever wanted to set out on an adventure—on a path of amazing experiences—just turn the page. Like Frodo, Harry, and Dorothy, you're about to discover the magic hidden inside of you . . . that has been there all along.

PART I

IMPROVING EFFECTIVENESS IN YOURSELF

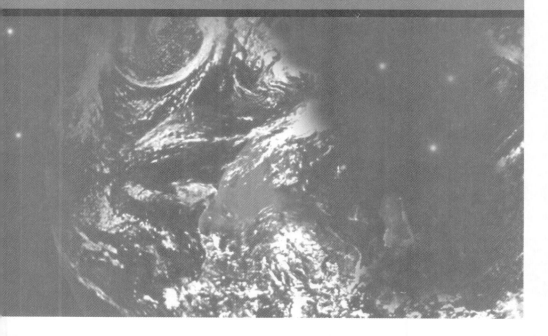

Author's Note: Whenever I ask you, the reader, to write things down as part of an exercise, the intention is that you do so on a separate piece of paper.

CHAPTER 1

PATTERN BUSTING

*"Insanity: doing the same thing over and
over again and expecting different results."*
— Albert Einstein

This was Jeffrey's third job in five years. Each time he started with high hopes, but he always seemed to find the organization wanting, his boss unsupportive, and his co-workers difficult. As he vented about work over dinner one night, his girlfriend asked him why he didn't confront the people who weren't giving him what he wanted. As he almost choked on his fish, he told her that no one cared and that he didn't want to get fired.

The next morning both the alarm and her question went off insistently in his mind as he woke up. He hit the snooze button on both. By the time he arrived at work, he'd organized a tidy out-basket of excuses that didn't improve his mood. Staring at his computer screen, he felt the start of a familiar headache. Jeffrey was trapped in a nightmare of the working dead but didn't know how to escape.

He slowly realized that he was in so much pain that anything had to be better. Somehow that thought was liberating, so when his boss called him into a meeting, he felt a strange detachment. As the discussion kicked off, Jeffrey surprised himself by speaking up and debating with his co-workers. He noticed people listening to him and treating him differently. At the end of the meeting, his boss sought him out, asking him to expand on his thoughts. As Jeffrey returned to his cubicle, it looked less like a prison. He knew that something at work had changed when *he* changed.

Jeffrey remembered how infinite and mysterious life had seemed when he was a child, and a young, adventurous feeling stirred within him. As he recalled games of pirates, dragon slayers, and warriors, he made a promise to the boy he used to be: "I'll find a way to bring your dreams to life. I won't let fear drive you away. Give me your sword, my friend. I'm tired of playing dead!"

Getting Off Automatic Pilot

Like Jeffrey, many of us spend our lives habitually repeating the same behavior—which may not work but feels comfortable. After 27 years as a therapist and communication consultant, being witness to many difficult relationships, I've learned that there are two kinds of suffering: necessary and unnecessary. The former is discomfort that reminds us of what we can't control and teaches us compassion. It may be comforting to know that no matter how many self-help books you read, life sometimes sucks anyway. Unnecessary pain, on the other hand, stems from repeated rituals of behavior that never seem to yield positive results. Despite the popular myth that suffering is part of being noble, suffering unnecessarily as a result of staying in bad situations isn't spiritual . . . it's silly and in some cases, plain stupid.

Much needless anguish is created when we act like zombies and repeat *social spells* learned early on from parents, friends, or society. Social spells are patterns of behavior we habitually repeat that feel comfortable, safe, and "normal." They're also ways that we try to influence others or get what we want. Many social spells we've learned don't work, but do feel "normal" and automatic. For instance, if our parents blamed other people when they were anxious, we might pick up this behavior, too. Predictably, people will feel bad around us in the same way we felt bad around our parents. We then repeat these patterns as we get divorced, lose jobs, and give up on our dreams. The sad part is that we created these losses without knowing that we had other options.

We constantly make assumptions about other people from the minute we meet them. If we're intuitive, some of what we make up may be true. Then again, much of what we concoct is influenced by what we fear, what we want, or what we deny about ourselves. We usually expect other people to react and behave like the first individuals we encounter—our family members. If Dad never thought we were good enough, we automatically assume that other people view us as inadequate. And we do this without much data to back it up. The only way to break out of being on automatic pilot is to be aware that our assumptions about people may be wrong.

For example, when one of my good friends, Marie, first met her husband, Bruce, she made assumptions about him based on *her* childhood. When Marie was born, her parents were locked in a bitter, violent, and unrewarding marriage. They were young, unprepared for parenthood, and unable to meet their own needs—let alone their children's. Both had rocky upbringings themselves. Marie's maternal grandparents and extended family were severe alcoholics, her father's dad was hospitalized for manic depression, and his mother died when he was young. Her father's older siblings, who were busy with their own families, raised her dad. Both of Marie's parents also struggled with different forms of mental illness. The needs of their three small children overwhelmed and sometimes even enraged them.

While dating Bruce, Marie was frequently upset with him because she *assumed* that he didn't care about her needs. Fortunately, Bruce didn't take her assumptions personally. Instead, he consistently showed her that he *did* care. One day after a year of dating, Bruce was late for an important event. Marie started her "zombie trance" by complaining that obviously her needs weren't important to him and he didn't think about her enough. Bruce didn't try to explain why he was late or try to defend himself. He simply gazed at Marie with unmistakable love and deep concern, and then said, "Sweetheart, I think of you in everything I do."

As she looked into his eyes, Marie knew that what he said was absolutely true. Bruce woke Marie out of her trance because he picked the right moment and the right words to reach her. It was only then that she was able to see through the *spell* of her childhood assumptions. Not long after, Bruce proposed and Marie accepted.

Whenever we enter into any professional or personal relationship, we unconsciously begin defending ourselves from the pain and anxiety we expect to occur as a result of past experiences. We're not interested in letting new people know us until we feel we can trust them. By the time we arrive at that place of trust, however, we've already made assumptions about who they are. We don't want to ask questions, reveal vulnerability, or risk rejection—even if we think we don't like the other person!

Using the language of Social Sorcery starts by noticing when we're slipping into automatic pilot so that we can choose to stop using the same social spells and conjure up new and improved patterns of behavior. There are still times when I find it challenging to know the right words, or to stay open rather than putting up defenses. Effective communication becomes easier over time, but it's rarely effortless. Being defensive, telling other people they're wrong, and withdrawing is easy.

When you break yourself (or others) out of trances, you're more likely to get your way, find creative solutions, and enjoy people. You'll find that every person you meet, even briefly, can give you information helpful to your success and well-being.

I recall a chance encounter with a stranger in London. It was a sunny day in spring when everything was blooming. I was marching with grim determination down the street, silently rehearsing the speech I'd be delivering at a conference. I hadn't noticed how tense and anxious I was until a gentleman walking in the other direction looked me in the eyes and gently said, "Smile." Suddenly I remembered that I was in a city I loved, that it was a beautiful day, and that I was excited about meeting people at the conference.

I had no doubt that the universe had lined up a brief moment with a complete stranger to remind me to be *alive* to the gift of that city and that day.

Now I'm going to introduce you to the first of my highly effective toolkits where you get to apply the language and strategies of Social Sorcery to your unique situations. You're welcome to make notes in the book, write your thoughts in a separate notebook, or just make mental notes in your head. If you and a friend are reading this together, you can use the toolkits in each chapter as an opening to find creative solutions to challenges in your work and home life. You can even get your book club to read it or start a Social Sorcery support group using these toolkits to transform the lives of group members.

Toolkit for Getting Off Automatic

1. What negative patterns can you see in your relationships (for example, betrayal, abandonment, or criticism)?

2. How do you repeatedly react?

3. Do these patterns remind you of any situation(s) in your family?

4. Think of a behavior you've never tried. What might happen if you tried it?

5. List relationships you have where you'd like more influence or connection.

6. List the assumptions you have about these people (for example, "They don't like me").

7. Ask yourself where you came up with this assumption. Was it someone's behavior, their words, or was it just a guess on your part?

8. Take the risk to ask about your assumption (that is, "Were you upset when I was late?").

An Example of Getting Off Automatic

Ted used this toolkit to get off automatically being taken advantage of by his boss. He started by noticing that he often felt "used" in his relationships. He'd usually just try to be more helpful, hoping he'd eventually be appreciated. He was stuck in a pattern of acting like a doormat, which started in his childhood when he took care of his alcoholic mom and dad. A behavior he'd never tried before was asking for what he wanted, because he was afraid people would see him as too demanding, perhaps even too needy.

With this toolkit, Ted could see that he'd *assumed* his boss would fire him if he asked for anything. So for a change he told his boss, "I'm interested in being promoted to a supervisor position within the next 12 months. What specific performance do you need from me so I can move into management?" As he continued to be assertive, his boss came to respect him, and indeed, Ted was promoted just six months later.

We can't break out of our zombie trances if we don't understand the emotional engines that drive our behavior. Our relationships are limited by our self-knowledge because our communication with others echoes the way we communicate with ourselves.

The parts of us that are socially acceptable and positive are easy to discover and admit to. Then there are the parts of us that are socially unacceptable, ugly, or cruel—those, of course, are difficult to acknowledge. If we consider ourselves to be spiritual, our vengeance, selfishness, or anger can make us feel particularly bad. These feelings, however, simply prove that we're human. Being on a spiritual path doesn't mean that we never have the urge to be mean or cruel; it simply means that we don't act on those urges.

We can't get to know parts of us that we refuse to acknowledge or that we judge as unworthy of our attention. If we're busy ignoring or judging our feelings, we don't articulate them. A good friend of mine, Sandy, was once walking down a street in Manila in the Philippines on a hot summer night with her husband, Dave. Sandy was terrified of the small groups of men who were standing on the sidewalk, so she wanted to walk in the street. Her husband, Dave, was also afraid because the crazy traffic in the street made him nervous. Instead of admitting their fears, they started to criticize each other and fight about where to walk. Finally, when they both realized that they were anxious, they started to laugh and hailed a taxi. How much easier it would have been to find a solution if they had both talked about how frightened they were at the *beginning* of the walk.

When we judge our reactions, we cast bad social spells because we don't know, don't ask, and don't get what we need. Insight and judgment can't occupy the same emotional space. If we don't realize that we're sad, we can't ask for comfort. If we don't know that we're angry, we can't figure out what's frustrating us. If we don't ask for what we want from others, we resent what other people need from us. We can continually change jobs, partners, or cities, but we still won't be happy if we can't tell people what we want. As many spiritual teachers have suggested, "Wherever you go, there you are," which means . . . "changing our environment doesn't change who we are."

Finding the Lost Self

If, as a child, your parents skillfully taught you how to express your needs, you're lucky—and unusual. Most children are taught to hide the truth about how they feel, or to keep what they think to themselves if it makes their parents uncomfortable.

Sadly, adults often motivate children by using shame, scolding, or criticism. In the end, neither parent nor child wins this battle. I remember my mother insisting that I eat my brussels sprouts with the usual reminder of starving children in other parts of the world. I believe that she was hoping to motivate me to chow down my vegetables by making me appreciate my good fortune. At first I felt like a bad, insensitive child as I continued to push my veggies around my plate. Then I got an idea. I generously suggested, "Let's send my vegetables to those poor kids!" In the end, my mother's desire for me to eat healthy food and my desire to avoid gagging on the dreaded vegetables left us in a permanent stalemate.

Many families repeat this scenario of power struggles over food night after night. The parents want the children to eat healthfully, and the kids want power and control over their bodies. If more parents realized that there's room for both parties to win, eating disorders would be less common. With my daughter, my husband and I have successfully used a trick involving what we call "smart food," where she gets the power and we get her to eat well. When she started eating solid foods, we labeled certain things "smart food" and told her that this was for parents. We told her that if children ate smart food, they got clever and figured out how to get what they wanted from their mom and dad.

Of course, we didn't want her to be *too* smart and get everything she wanted, so we begged her to please *avoid* smart food. We then placed fruits, veggies, or anything else she hadn't tried just out of her reach and "accidentally" turned our backs just long enough for her to put the food on her plate. After she ate the smart food, we attributed anything we normally would have done for her to her ultimate cleverness in making us do what she wanted. If we made her cookies, arranged a playdate, or took her swimming—you can be sure that we blamed smart food. She's now seven, and aware that we want her to eat good food, but she just *loves* the feeling of controlling her parents. So she gets to have the power, and we get her to eat a varied, nutritionally sound diet.

Children are passionate creatures who are nonverbal, socially unskilled, and impulsive. Their emotional volatility can be seen when they express undying hatred for a mom or dad one minute and smother the parent with hugs the next. Little people just don't know yet how to manage, understand, or express their emotions. So if you were shamed for being angry, selfish, or sensitive, you may spend a lifetime trying to hide these unacceptable feelings. You may not realize that the grown-ups who did this shaming didn't get much emotional education either, and your honest expressiveness made them uncomfortable. Lots of us were also hit, yelled at, or called names when we were just being honest. Our parents threatened: "I'll give you something to cry about!" or "Wipe that look off your face" or "Don't make me spank you!" Usually these were the messages their parents gave *them*. Children can be loved, but still end up carrying emotional handicaps from parents who don't have the skills or motivation to do better.

When we bury emotional reactions that are unacceptable to our parents, we lose information critical to our well-being. As children, we don't realize that our parents can't see everything that's going on inside of our heads. Thus, we hide information about how we're feeling from ourselves so Mom and Dad can't see it. By the time we become adults, hiding these emotions is automatic, and we can no longer fully access our hearts or souls.

Some psychologists, such as Alice Miller, believe that children create a false self to avoid rejection. This false self replaces the authentic self so well that many grown-ups forget who they really are. In my family, it was made clear that none of us children were supposed to be selfish. As a child, I went to great lengths to avoid looking out for, or thinking about, myself. For a great deal of my adult life, I also didn't take good care of myself. Of course, being human, from time to time I *was* selfish. I usually couldn't evaluate if my selfishness was useful or not because I assumed *all* selfishness was bad. I was also easy to manipulate since I'd bend over backward to do what someone else wanted if they called me selfish.

One time when I was a young adult, my mom used a familiar social spell in our family and called me "selfish." The usual result of this spell was that my sisters and I would do anything my mom wanted immediately after she accused us of this. Now this was after I'd had a fair amount of therapy. It suddenly dawned on me that coming from *this* family and being *capable* of being selfish was quite an achievement. As I mulled this over, I looked calmly at my mom and said, "Thank you for seeing that I'm selfish sometimes. I'm happy to have a time in my life without anyone else to take care of. I appreciate your acknowledgment." My mom looked surprised, then confused, and never called me selfish again.

I broke the emotional *hold* of this word when I looked to myself to evaluate my behavior. As I stopped giving my mother the power to define my behavior, I was able to act differently than she expected. I was also able to see that I had been my mom's "caretaker" from the time I was a young child. It made sense to me that my mother might be angry when I stopped taking care of her and starting taking care of myself. Defining my behavior as "bad" allowed her to make her disappointment *my* fault and not reveal her own need for my care. My mother had been equally trapped in the spell of the word *selfish*. She had simply passed on to me what her mother had taught her.

When the people who are supposed to care for us can't or don't acknowledge our emotional life, two things can happen:

1. We learn to hide our feelings, thoughts, and needs even from ourselves, because as children we believe that adults know everything we're thinking.

2. We never learn to identify what we're feeling because people around us don't help us label our emotions, or model how to deal with feelings effectively.

Frank, one of my clients, told me that he was being "weak and pathetic" during a time when he was avoiding his family. I asked Frank if he was sure he was weak and pathetic, or maybe he was starting to be aware of how afraid he was around his family. He looked confused, and then it occurred to Frank that his family had defined his fear as pathetic. Parents are the gods and goddesses of a child's limited world. They tell us when we're tired, when we're hungry, and what the word *car* means—they also provide our first emotional dictionary.

All of us lose some portion of our true self in childhood. Even if our parents are accepting, our friends, our teachers, and other important people may have disapproved of our reactions. Eventually, we disown pieces of our soul in our efforts to win the love and approval of others. Our feelings seem dangerous if we express them and get rejected.

Training the Heart

Most parents know that kids don't naturally know how to swim, so they give their children lessons. If a parent just throws a kid in the water, they'll usually end up with a child who has water phobias for life. Most parents believe that since talking is natural, talking about emotions is natural as well. However, kids who get thrown into emotions without help get phobias about going anywhere near feelings. Emotions are no more dangerous than water, but both swimming and communicating require adequate training.

You can see the lack of natural communication skills when you watch small children having conflicts. When my daughter first formed friendships as a preschooler, the common accusation was: "You're mean!" I kept pointing out to my daughter and her friends that saying "You're mean" provides no *information* other than blame. Over time, my daughter and her buddies realized the power inherent in stating what they *wanted* instead of calling each other "mean."

If our emotional lessons never go beyond feeling that others are mean, we may no longer know what we want, how to ask for it, or how to enjoy it if we got it. My friend Judy Long-Severance wrote a poem that illustrates the difficulty of remembering what we want:

Why I Don't Know What I Want

If I wanted something
    (which I don't know if I do),
    I wouldn't tell you what it was
    anyway, because you probably
    wouldn't give it to me (or it
    might not be the same thing
    you wanted, so we'd have to
    argue about it).
Then, if I won and got my way,
    I wouldn't want it (because I'd
    know what I want And there
    are so many ways it could go
    wrong if I did know).
It's probably better this way.
    (anyway, I expect you prob-
    ably think so).

When our hearts haven't been "trained" and we disown parts of ourselves, we go through life as if we have one hand tied behind our back. The buried pieces of our soul contain talents, creativity, and intuitive skills that we need to guide us. We may gradually lose all sense of our true self as we move through adult life—a bad marriage or a difficult job can obliterate any fragile connection we still have to our true selves. Many folks new to my coaching or therapy practice can't even tell me what they want or how they feel.

If you look for your real self, you'll discover a treasure chest of creativity, new options, and even new allies under what may look like muddy, uncomfortable feelings. For instance, when I do mediation in corporations, I find that the people most at loggerheads with each other are those who share the same emotional challenges. After a successful mediation, former enemies often form strong alliances based on new understandings of common issues. We often don't realize that most people who annoy us have similar vulnerabilities.

Another good example of finding the lost self and training the heart can be seen in the movie *Jerry Maguire*. The title character, played by Tom Cruise, starts out as an emotionally disconnected, big-time sports agent who feels that his work is meaningless. He realizes that he hates himself and his life. Late one evening at a professional conference, he connects with his deepest self and in a creative frenzy writes a mission statement called "The Things We Think and Do Not Say: The Future of Our Business," which emphasizes personal connections with clients. In the middle of the night, he distributes the statements to the mail slots at the hotel. When he wakes up, he get nervous and tries to pull the documents, but everyone is already reading them. As he exits the elevator into the lobby and people from his office see him, he looks like he might dash back in . . . then the applause begins.

The movie shows how training his heart and finding his soul lead Jerry to fulfill his deepest desires at work and in love. In that moment when his co-workers applaud, it's because he's connected to the best in everyone by reconnecting to himself. By the end of the movie, Jerry is practicing Social Sorcery.

Toolkit for Training the Heart

1. What messages about emotions do you remember hearing as a child?

2. What feelings do you believe are not acceptable or spiritual (for example, jealousy)?

3. When do you feel these emotions, and what do you do?

4. How often do you have no idea how you feel?

An Example of Training the Heart

Jenna remembered hearing her mother tell her what a bad, ungrateful child she was whenever she was angry. She also had a physically violent father who hurt her, her mother, and her brothers when he was enraged. She decided that anger was destructive, and only evil people expressed this emotion. She often didn't notice when she was mad, but she did have an enormous problem with her weight. When Jenna used this toolkit, she realized that she'd often eat when she was feeling angry. By noticing that she was feeling this emotion before she hit the Ben & Jerry's ice cream, she had the option to call friends or write in her journal to express her frustrations. For the first time in her life, she was able to lose weight and keep it off.

Like Jenna, many people get the idea that anger is a "bad" emotion and that mature people should not feel or express it. In many families and in our culture, forgiveness is celebrated, but anger is vilified. Obviously, biting or hitting other people is an inappropriate way to express anger, but this emotion in itself is an example of raw, inspiring energy. Many adults go to great lengths and much self-destructive behavior to avoid feeling angry. Women often overeat, men drink, and certain people get even, not mad. Some people may even end up with physical symptoms like migraines (blowing their top), stomach problems, or back problems rather than admitting how they feel.

I've worked with a few highly successful clients who came from crazy, violent families and who might have naturally ended up in institutions themselves. When I've asked how they turned out so well, they always give me the same answer: "I got mad, and it saved my life." In the last decade, there's been much research on something called "resiliency," which means extraordinary mental health in people who had truly rotten starts in life. The research has found that one of the critical attributes shared by resilient people is the ability to get angry as motivation for escaping destructive family patterns.

As you get off automatic and start training your heart, you'll discover a new level of freedom that you've never experienced before. Let's use this new freedom in the next chapter to exorcise the ghosts of your past so that you can attain the life you long for.

CHAPTER 2

BANISHING FAMILY "GHOSTS"

"It's never too late to be what you might have been."
— George Eliot

Most of us can think of several bitter moments in our personal history. And for some of us, childhood was a special hell all its own. But self-pity isn't an excuse to stay stuck as an adult. People who choose to feel sorry for themselves are refusing to take accountability for their current circumstances. They deny uncomfortable self-truths, and the subsequent lies they tell themselves keep them trapped. In fact, only children are *truly* victims of circumstance. All adults, regardless of their history, can create a new future with every breath they take.

Making Lemonade Out of Lemons

The difficulties of childhood can actually be perceived as a training ground for many of the talents people possess as adults. Joseph Campbell, author and mythology expert, once said that we should pity those who had no wounds because our gift comes from our wound, and those with no wound have no gift.

During the Middle Ages, it was believed that one could create gold out of base metal. Early scientists involved in this pursuit were called alchemists. Over time, alchemy has been used as a metaphor for the spiritual development of human beings. Taking our wounds and transforming them into our gifts was seen as the soul work of each person.

No one would choose to put an innocent child through a painful situation, yet we've all survived less-than-optimal families. Grieving our losses, facing our disappointments, and acknowledging our rage is the key to escaping the repetition of our childhood experiences as adults. When one of my clients finally saw how she kept re-creating her family patterns, she joked, "Wait a minute! You mean the world isn't my mother?" Distilling gifts from our painful experiences frees us from waiting for our families to change and give us what they can't. As adults, we can then recognize and walk away from other adults who can't give us what we need either.

For those of us who had dramatically crazy, violent, or addictive families, extraordinary abilities are often waiting under the rubble of childhood misery. Amazing intuition, unusual insight, and keen empathy can be the capacities these children developed *because they had to.* Many of my clients tell me that their drive to succeed, help people, or create beauty was forged out of intensely painful childhood experiences.

This doesn't mean that it's fine and dandy if you went through hell as a kid because of all those goodies you can now claim. "I did the best I could" is not a useful phrase for any child to hear from either of their parents, because even parents who really try will still fail their children in significant ways. The most comforting words for a child of any age who's dealing with parental shortcomings is to hear them say, "I know I let you down sometimes. I love you, and I want to know how you felt. I also want to know what you need from me now."

Children often see their parents as all-powerful and Divine. When parents can tolerate their kids' anger or frustration, these children learn to accept *their* own powerlessness. Parents who refuse to listen to their kids' expressions of disappointment because they can't stand to feel inadequate only succeed in alienating them.

In alchemy, the base metal had to be exposed to intense heat to complete the transformation into gold. In Social Sorcery, the extreme heat is provided by the emotional intensity that accompanies relationships. It's natural to avoid what we find uncomfortable, but it makes us slaves to our history. If we want to break the chains of childhood and find our gifts, the admission price is remembering the feelings of the kid that was left behind. People who don't remember their history are in a permanent emotional version of the film *Groundhog Day,* trapped in virtually the same difficulties over and over again.

When my clients start the journey to find the gifts in their childhood, they often feel anxious about what they're *not.* As they enter the middle phases, they fear what they'll find out about who they really are. On the final legs of the journey, my clients are surprised to find that they already are . . . who they always longed to be . . . but just didn't know they were.

Toolkit for Making Lemonade Out of Lemons

1. What was most painful to you during your childhood?

2. In what area do you have the most interests or talents as an adult?

3. What connection do you see between your pain and your gifts?

An Example of Creating Lemonade Out of Lemons

Jacob thought that the most painful part of his childhood was that his parents seemed too caught up in their own lives to notice him. He felt invisible and like an inconvenience to them.

As an adult, Jacob was a top-selling salesperson with an amazing knack for figuring out what people wanted. When he used this tool, he could see that he'd developed his extraordinary skill for reading people as a kid, when he tried to figure out how to make his parents happy with him. Jacob now celebrates his lucrative sales skills as the lemonade derived out of the sour disappointment of not having more attentive or empathetic parents.

Creating Extraordinary Effectiveness Through "Mystical Abnormality"

Having the Interpersonal Edge will make you extraordinarily and *abnormally* effective because most people operate in ways that are familiar but not very magical. Our tendency is to repeat the normal and safe patterns we learned in our families even if the results we create are painful for us. When Lily Tomlin said that reality is just "a collective hunch," she was pointing out that an idea can be highly popular, in our families or society, without that concept necessarily being true. When you have the Interpersonal Edge, you realize that normalcy is highly overrated, and abnormality can be a mystical experience where you think outside the box and find flexible solutions in order to get what you want.

I enjoy teasing my corporate and therapy clients with the promise that they'll be "mystically abnormal" after working with me. When one of my clients, Briana, was worried about drinking too much and putting herself in dangerous situations, we discussed the option of her not drinking for a while. Briana looked worried and said, "But Dr. Skube, everybody drinks a lot. It's *normal!*" I chuckled and asked her why she was working with me if she was committed to being normal. We both laughed, and Briana added, "I'll settle for mystical abnormality and better results, then."

Milton Erickson, a highly talented therapist, was known for refusing to write down his innovative theories. When badgered by his students to explain why his methods were so effective, he'd only say, "Most people are a little too rigid." He was emphasizing that the person with the most flexible set of options in a difficult situation will have the best chance to find a solution.

If we stop trying new approaches because we feel inadequate, don't want to look foolish, or are operating on automatic pilot, we're limiting our possibilities. Mystical abnormality means that we choose getting the result we want over being right, being comfortable, or looking good.

For instance, one of my corporate clients, Juan, wanted to be promoted but was afraid to draw attention to himself. He came in for corporate coaching because he felt taken advantage of and unappreciated. Although he was bright and hardworking, Juan came from a family where drawing attention to oneself was punished severely. As we explored his dilemma, I asked who made it possible for bosses and co-workers to take him for granted. Juan looked confused and finally managed, "Well . . . I guess *I* do." My client could have remained a victim of circumstances bemoaning his ungrateful environment, but instead, he chose mystical abnormality, stopped being a "normal" doormat, and got his promotion.

We can easily revert to old habits despite our best intentions. My clients find it most annoying when they know better and act normal anyway. I urge them, "Be patient with yourself. You've been acting normal for several decades, and it takes awhile to change habits. If you blow it, congratulate yourself; you now know one more thing that doesn't work."

It also isn't cheating to go *back* into a situation after blowing it. I, for instance, can be a tad touchy about being criticized. My husband may ask where I put the peanut butter when I'm having a weak "normal" moment, and I'll say, "Hey—you try organizing the pantry!" because I figure he's judging my kitchen-management skills. If he looks puzzled and informs me that he merely wanted a peanut-butter sandwich, then I realize that I was acting out of my zombie trance. I then act mystically abnormal, mutter "Oops," tell him I thought he was criticizing me, and make amends by happily helping him find what he was looking for.

Nobody is mystically abnormal all the time. Even Buddha and Jesus are reported to have had their weak "normal" moments. *Normal* encompasses habits such as defending yourself when criticized, trying to change other people, and ignoring problems. These behaviors won't lead to any spiritual breakthroughs; they're simply "business as usual." *Abnormal* means that you choose curiosity over being right, ask questions rather than make assumptions, and try new things that would normally scare you.

Bob, one of my clients, is the CEO of a large software company. In working with him, I discovered that his parents had humiliated him whenever he felt nervous. As an adult, Bob acted certain even when it was obvious he was confused. He also attacked others when they pointed out that he *seemed* uncertain, because this made him feel embarrassed. When people tried to support him, he wouldn't accept the help because he felt ashamed of his fear. His anxiety triggered an automatic trance, where he acted in current situations as if others were his parents.

Before I worked with Bob, there were two major consequences to his behavior: Employees in the company didn't feel safe asking questions, and they acted like they knew what they were doing even when they had no idea. For example, everyone pretended to understand how to produce software, or avoided admitting that they were having problems. The employees would wait for one team to crack and confess their confusion, or worse, be found out by the customer. Then everyone would blame the team that admitted feeling confused. The blamed team lost status in the organization, heads rolled, and the game of chicken started all over again. The morale and productivity of the entire organization declined with every round.

Another negative result was that Bob's employees were reluctant to support him by offering help or direction. My client felt isolated and alienated, even from his management team.

After a couple of sessions with him, I was able to show Bob that *he* was the main person who thought something was wrong with him if he didn't have all the answers. He was also able to see the connection between the way his parents had reacted when he was afraid and how he believed everyone would react now. Bob was so spellbound by his past that he couldn't see the current moment. After my coaching, he was able to create a corporate culture where people could ask questions, his management team and employees began supporting him, and productivity and morale soared.

✦ O ✦

The adage "Be here now" is common and practical spiritual advice. We can't be effective in the now if we're still spellbound by our history.

Sometimes we get glimpses that our knee-jerk patterns aren't getting us what we want, and we vow to change them. We swear to treat our children better than we were treated, then find ourselves channeling our parents. We pledge to speak up for ourselves, but go silent when an opportune moment to speak arrives. We promise not to blow up again, and next time we're mad, we imitate a volcano.

Changing our "normal" patterns can take longer than we think it should. Terry, one of my therapy clients, had been particularly frustrated by his inability to change. After a few sessions with me, he surprised himself by suddenly breaking out of several painful patterns at work. As he was reveling in his newfound freedom, Terry observed, "Therapy is inconvenient and unsettling . . . and way, way better than the alternative."

To practice mystical abnormality, we need to recognize what's true for us; otherwise, we'll get into big fights with people where we need them to agree with our viewpoint. Think of it this way: Gravity is a law of nature. It doesn't get into arguments with people who don't believe in it; it just pulls them to the ground. If you believe in gravity and people want to argue with you, let them win the argument. As they get older, they may come to notice gravity, and if not, you can still set up *your* life to cooperate with nature.

Toolkit for Creating Extraordinary Effectiveness Through Mystical Abnormality

1. Notice what you always do in an annoying situation that you want to change.

2. List in your head or on paper, actions or words that would feel abnormal.

3. Identify what you'd be afraid of if you tried something new.

4. Is what you're afraid of any worse than what you're already experiencing?

5. Write down a new action that you could take to produce a new result.

An Example of Creating Extraordinary Effectiveness

Angela noticed that she became critical of others at work when she was nervous. She didn't see the result until her co-workers had withdrawn or blown up at her. She realized that it would feel highly abnormal to her to let them know she was worried, but she was afraid that people at work would think she was immature. Angela laughed out loud after doing this toolkit because she saw that her co-workers already thought she was childish because of her intense criticism. She was astonished that her fellow employees actually offered to help her when she admitted concern about work projects and stopped criticizing.

Truth or Telepathy?

When we're young, we know what's true about ourselves. For example, we proudly proclaim, "Broccoli tastes yucky," "I want a pony," or "I don't want to share." However, we don't know how to tell the truth *skillfully.* We might get a present we don't like and broadcast, "I hate Etch A Sketch!" We aren't told that it's okay to not like the present, but we still need to say "Thank you." In other instances, we get so frustrated trying to tell the truth that we give up and say what we *think* people want to hear.

People often confuse feelings and behavior. Children are better off if they're taught that *any* feeling is okay, and then shown the best words to express their reactions. Instead, what usually happens is that both the feelings *and* the words get rejected. As children, when we don't get lessons in translating raw emotions into useful language, we genuinely don't know what to say, so we often lie. By the time we grow up, it has become habitual to lie, defend ourselves, and try to look good.

The problem with lying is that we get so proficient at it that we forget the truth. The truth is like a large ocean wave with enormous spiritual power: We can ride it or dive into it, but we can't outswim it. However, knowing the truth doesn't mean blurting it out at the company party; it's simply an internal acknowledgment of reality. If your friend asks you if her dress makes her look fat, no one wins if you say yes. One truth may be that the dress makes her look fat. Yet another equally accurate response would be to say you like the color, or you think that another dress is more flattering.

I've seen people who make a "religion" out of honesty and use truth as a weapon. These people are seldom well liked or successful. There's a difference between being honest and being insensitive. We don't have to verbalize every thought we think. We often have thoughts or feelings that are fleeting, unfair, or cruel. There's probably a good reason that telepathy isn't common. We all want to be understood and heard, but it's important to know when, where, and how to speak the truth. It actually requires more skill to tell the truth well than to lie craftily.

To speak honestly, we have to know what we think or feel. If we get anxious when our partner drives fast and we blurt out, "You're crazy and reckless!" no message is received, only blame. Blaming language triggers defensive reactions in others. If, instead, we talk about our anxiety when our partner drives fast (for example, "I'm beginning to feel nervous—could you please slow down a little?"), our partner will be more likely to give us what we want. Obviously, if our partner *still* doesn't listen, we can make different choices in the future, such as not being in a car when this person drives.

Invoking Self-Reflection

To avoid blurting out the first thing that comes into your head, Social Sorcery requires self-reflection, which is a pause that truly refreshes, because you take a moment to consider your choices before reacting automatically. Let's say that your secretary is making too many typos. When you threw a fit as a kid, your parents caved in. Since then you've learned that getting angry scares people and they give you what you want. Thus, you yell at your secretary about the errors. He continues to make mistakes, so you yell louder. As his errors increase, you continue to bellow, believing that eventually he'll shape up. Finally, he quits and you're faced with finding a replacement.

If you'd invoked self-reflection, you would have considered options other than yelling. You could have asked if he was overloaded or needed help rearranging priorities. You could have told him calmly that error-free work was more important than other objectives. You could have set up rewards or consequences for what you wanted, and you wouldn't now have to interview for a new secretary.

When you use self-reflection, you quickly brainstorm for the best option rather than repeating old, unsuccessful patterns. I can tell when my executive-coaching or therapy clients are making progress on self-reflection because they often do *nothing*. They know that their old patterns won't work, and they don't know what else to do.

For example, my client Marissa managed to have a calm

dinner with her husband even though she was furious with him. She came in for our next session and said, "I'm thrilled. I sat there fuming, but I didn't do anything destructive. I was fully aware of all the things I normally do and how they never work." We were then able to figure out the words and behavior for her to use to discuss what she wanted with her husband.

Here's a tip to help you with self-reflection: Remember the words *stop, drop,* and *roll.* Early in my career, I worked as an education coordinator, and one of the areas I taught was fire safety. I was amazed to learn that most people don't know what to do if they catch on fire, so they run around in a panic fanning the flames. Most people react similarly when a relationship is "on fire."

If you were to actually catch on fire, *stop, drop,* and *roll* are buzzwords to remind you to react in a way that puts the fire out. And, if your relationship is in flames, the same buzzwords for self-reflection apply: *Stop* the old, immediate negative response, *drop* into yourself for a moment of reflection, then *roll* out the new response (considering options and selecting the most powerful alternative).

If we stick with the devil we know, we can definitely feel like victims of black magic. A student of mine, George, was a busy guy. He worked 60 hours a week, ran daily, and was active in his church. His wife was also independent and active. He felt lonely, and frequently fought with his wife about wanting more attention. When he *stopped* blaming his wife, he saw that he repeatedly created situations where he felt unloved and lonely. When he *dropped* into his feelings, George noticed that he felt stifled and controlled whenever his wife asked to spend time with him. He started to see that he was fiercely independent because he was afraid of rejection. He was then able to *roll* out a new response. He let his wife know that he missed her and wanted to make time to be together. If he hadn't learned to *stop, drop,* and *roll,* his marriage might have burned down while he acted "normal."

When people find themselves in repetitive, painful situations, it's because they've fallen into a pattern that hides their deepest fears. It's ironic that we keep avoiding the same emotional experience we've already gone through and survived. I've watched many people *running on fire* through their days determined to outrun their past as their rich potential lives burn to ashes in their frenetic flight from fear. Most of the damage we inflict when we refuse to *stop, drop,* and *roll* isn't due to the fire; it's because we're more afraid of change than suffering.

Toolkit for Invoking Self-Reflection

1. *Stop* and remember the last time you felt uncomfortable in a difficult situation.

2. *Drop* into the feelings that accompanied the situation.

3. *Roll* out different actions or words you could have used.

An Example of Invoking Self-Reflection

Harry had an exciting new project that he wanted to head up. Instead, his boss gave it to a co-worker. He normally would have believed that his boss thought he wasn't talented enough and would have proceeded to plot a campaign of revenge against her. Instead he *stopped* plotting, *dropped* into himself, and noticed his automatic vengeful response: He was ready to hang his boss without a trial. Next, he *rolled* out a new response. He asked her what the reasons were behind the project assignment and inquired about other projects she wanted him to work on. He felt pretty foolish when he found out that a better project was being assigned to him. He realized that he would have missed out on this opportunity if he'd been busy getting even with his boss.

In corporate classes, I often joke with my new students, telling them that I'll know how successful I've been by how "abnormal" they feel by the end of our seminars. Now that I've got you feeling less haunted by your past, more mystically abnormal, and doing the new *stop, drop,* and *roll* dance, let's boogie to the next chapter and check out your Divine body.

CHAPTER 3

THE DIVINE BODY

*"He that has eyes to see and ears to hear may convince himself
that no mortal can keep a secret. If his lips are silent, he chatters
with his finger-tips; betrayal oozes out of him at every pore."*
— Sigmund Freud

Our culture ignores the fact that people have bodies and we use them to express meaning. When I teach nonverbal communication to organizations, even my executive students will giggle and look embarrassed. I chuckle to myself when "out-of-body" experiences are described as spiritually "advanced." A more uncommon spiritual experience for most folks would be one that's "in-the-body."

Power and Breathing

To tune in to your body, pay attention to your breath. Is it shallow, high in your chest, or down in your stomach? See how long you can stay aware of your breath as you read. You may even find yourself cursing when I remind you to breathe as you read this chapter. Noticing one's lack of awareness is an inherently annoying proposition.

By working to be conscious of both your breathing and your reading, you're training yourself to have a "two-track" mind. Most of us are only aware of our thinking during conversations. When we pay attention to our breathing, we expand our consciousness to include our physical feelings—and we can use our feelings to connect to our soul. Many spiritual disciplines encourage paying attention to the breath to connect to the spirit. When working with clients, I often have to remind them to breathe, because when people feel an uncomfortable emotion, they actually stop doing so. Clients tell me that even years after working with me, when they get uncomfortable, they can hear me saying "Breathe!"

Listening to Body Talk

When you have the Interpersonal Edge, you'll use all of yourself—mind, body, and soul—to relate to others. Your mind provides data, your heart provides emotion, and your spirit connects us to our Source. The soul speaks to you through your physical feelings, including your intuition. Even Einstein said that all his good ideas started as sensations in his body, and then he needed to translate them. If you ignore your body, or can't feel it, all the rich emotional and intuitive information it carries isn't available to you.

To explore how important your body is, imagine a pie chart that represents a total message being communicated. What percentage of the total chart would you assign to each of the following?

- Words
- Tone of voice
- Body language

If you made the guess that most people do, you gave words the largest percentage. Public speakers spend hours rehearsing what to say. In arguments, people bicker over exactly what *should* have been said. How many hours have you spent wondering what the perfect words would have been? However, consider this work by the social psychologist Albert Mehrabian. In a classic study of communication, he found the following answers to the question I just posed:

1. Words convey only 7 percent of the message.

2. Tone of voice accounts for 38 percent of what is understood by the listener.

3. Body language puts across a whopping 55 percent of the emotional meaning.

If you add it up, body and voice together convey 93 percent of the message. Blocking out people's words is often critical to understanding the soul of an interaction. *(Are you still paying attention to your breathing?)*

You've probably seen those books that feature a sexy woman or a handsome man on the cover, promising to teach you how to "know what he/she is really thinking." The truth is that there's no secret code. There are, however, a few common nonverbal signals in our culture (and I'm not talking about the rude gestures people make on the freeway).

When people nod their heads, they're usually interested in understanding your ideas—or are in agreement with you. If they're shaking their head side to side, they have concern or disagreement about what you're saying. If a person avoids eye contact, they may be shy or from a culture where direct eye contact is considered rude—or they may simply not want to interact with you. Open body posture usually suggests an interested person who wants to communicate with you. If someone turns away, they probably don't want to be dealing with you at that time.

Don't make automatic assumptions about body postures without checking out your theories. For example, when others cross their arms and lean away, they may want distance. They're probably withdrawing, but you won't know why unless you ask. They may disagree with you or be offended by something you've said, or maybe they just have to go to the bathroom. You might observe, "You leaned away and crossed your arms," or "Your voice got soft," or "You haven't looked at me since I told you I didn't like the project."

You'll often be surprised by the explanation. Once you experience a few surprises, you'll develop fewer theories and more curiosity. When this starts to happen, figuring out nonverbal clues will get easier for you. Remember, any person may be an exception to these guidelines, and there are many cultural and ethnic differences inherent in nonverbal communication.

When you point out "nonverbals" to people, it's like stripping them psychologically naked, because the body never lies. When dealing with someone who's defensive, ask questions without referring to any physical description. You can ask for information by saying, "I have the feeling," and then state your theory. For instance, "I have the feeling this isn't a good time to talk." With people who are less defensive, it's fine to describe behavior. For instance, you might say, "When you look away, I wonder if you're in a hurry." If in doubt, chalk up your observations to intuition.

Most body language is unique and idiosyncratic. If your boss is scratching her nose, it doesn't mean that she's lying—she may just have an itchy nose. If you consistently watch the body language of people around you, you'll develop a vocabulary for it. After a while, you'll notice consistencies—for example, whenever your boss is nervous, she tugs on her collar. Or, when your co-worker's mad, he rubs his neck. To develop this vocabulary, you'll need to maintain a two-track brain, taking note of nonverbal communication while remaining in conversation. *(Are you still paying attention to your breathing?)*

Toolkit for Listening to Body Talk

1. Turn on the TV and turn down the sound. What do you think people are feeling based on their expressions and gestures? Notice which gestures and expressions go together. To make this exercise more fun, call a friend and ask that person to turn on the same show with the sound just low enough so that *you* can't hear it. Tell your friend what emotion each character is expressing, and have him or her tell you whether or not you're right.

2. Next time you're at a boring social event, you'll have the perfect opportunity to focus on nonverbals. Notice those who are unlikely to engage you in interesting conversations and observe their nonverbal behavior. In particular, be aware of instances in which the nonverbal behavior and tone of voice doesn't fit the communication. In what way did the body language and words disagree?

3. Many of us waste years of our lives in boring meetings, but now that you're developing the Interpersonal Edge, you'll never experience another tedious conference because you'll be sharpening your skills in understanding body language. Business gatherings are full of confusing nonverbals. People are supposed to be involved and thoughtful, but how do they really look? Which people are truly engaged? How do you know this from their nonverbal behavior? How are others expressing their disinterest or impatience?

4. You can use a videotape to understand your nonverbal communication by recording your delivery of a short, passionate opinion, or record a conversation with someone on an interesting topic. For contrast, videotape yourself speaking on a subject you don't care about. Notice your facial expression, eye contact, posture, use of limbs, speed of movement, and the volume of your voice. Do you see anything on tape that you'd like to change?

5.   If you don't have access to a video recorder, ask a friend to observe your nonverbal behavior. Have this person watch you at a meeting or speaking in a group, and ask for feedback.

An Example of Listening to Body Talk

Raoul was watching the committee members in another long, boring meeting. He noticed that his boss leaned forward, tilted his head up, and uncrossed his arms whenever the subject of new marketing materials was raised. Raoul realized how interested his boss was in redesigning the current materials. After the meeting, he went into his boss's office and mentioned that he'd been thinking about a concept for new brochures and updating the Website. His boss sat up straight and complimented Raoul on his proactive offer. He put him in charge of this important new project, all because Raoul knew how to listen to body talk.

Building Rapport from Head to Toe

Some therapists use a technique called "entrainment" to achieve a deeper rapport with a client by matching the body language and the voice of the client. You can use this same tool when you want to establish trust, connection, or cooperation. If the person you're speaking with talks softly, rapidly, and with a low pitch, then you do the same. Matching the other person's tone of voice creates a feeling of connection and helps you understand their emotions. Or, if the person you're interacting with speaks quietly and slowly, you may feel calmer as you match that verbal style.

You can also match nonverbal actions. If Jane leans toward you, try leaning toward her. If she shrugs her shoulders frequently, experiment with that gesture. You'll not only express your interest in her through imitation, you'll also feel in your body what it's like to mimic her movements. Or, if a co-worker keeps her body posture closed and talks in a monotone and you mirror that behavior, you'll have more insight into her emotional state.

Do you feel bored when using a monotone voice, or depressed? Do you feel safer with a closed body posture, or defensive? Make sure your mirroring movements are subtle and don't match *every* movement, or people may think you're making fun of them.

Toolkit for Building Rapport

Ask a friend to be your partner in the following exercise: During a conversation, match or mirror the nonverbals of your friend. What do you learn about this person as you match movements? Ask your partner about his/her experience as you match nonverbals.

An Example of Building Rapport

Betina was dealing with a customer, Henry, whom everyone dreaded because he was touchy and demanding. Remembering the toolkit for creating rapport, she subtly started to mirror back his movements. As usual, he was ranting loudly and angrily about his rights as a customer. Betina planted her feet widely, clenched her jaw, and matched Henry's other movements while listening. She was astonished when she noticed that he was calming down, speaking softy, and thanking her for her help without her even speaking a word!

When Your Walk Doesn't Talk

(Are you still paying attention to your breathing?) Communication that conveys one message in words and another in tone and body language is called "incongruent." This type of communication makes the listener feel "crazy" and distant from the speaker.

That is, if my nonverbals are angry but I tell you that everything's okay, you won't know whether to respond to my words or my body language.

Research done on dysfunctional families has found that incongruent body and tone-of-voice messages can even drive people insane. At work, these same kinds of incongruent messages make employees feel stressed and unable to talk about the real issues. Most of us respond to the verbal part of the message, but are uneasy about incongruent, nonverbal signals. We learn early on to act as if we believe the words even though we may know that the nonverbal messages carry the truth. We can end up distrusting someone whose words *seem* friendly. We can feel insulted by someone who *said* nice things. We've all seen a stage magician focus the attention of the audience on his right hand while his left hand sets up the trick behind his back. Like the magician's audience members, we tend to focus on the words and miss the real action in the body language.

So make a point of noticing when other people's nonverbals—or your own—don't match. Then trust the body language, not the words. I once helped a client who was entrenched in a painful conflict with his wife to focus on his body language and ignore his words during our first session. He kept explaining how he loved his wife while pounding his fist on my table. As I was listening to him, I asked, while pounding my fist on the table, "Do you have any idea why your wife might think you're angry with her?" He then realized that he was communicating fury, not love, to his wife, and that their conflict couldn't clear up as long as he kept insisting he wasn't mad.

To make sense of incongruent communication, you have to *ask* the speaker about the mismatch between their verbal and nonverbal messages. But blurting out, "Hey, are ya trying to make me crazy—smiling while you criticize me?" isn't recommended. Instead, point out the mismatch with something like, "I notice you're smiling although you're telling me how disappointed you are in my work. I'm confused. Can you help me understand more clearly what you're telling me?" The speaker may say she feels uneasy telling you about her disappointment, or she may say that she doesn't want to discourage you. You can then talk about underlying issues rather than assuming that the person is trying to annoy you. Be aware that most of the time people aren't aware that they're sending mismatched messages.

Check out your incongruent messages as well, because they'll give you a wealth of information about your deeper self. I remember the first time I was videotaped doing a speech. When I watched the video later on, I was surprised to see a repetitious "dance." I would walk confidently around, stop, make a powerful point, and then shrug my shoulders. The nonverbal message I was sending was that I didn't know what I was talking about. After noticing my unconscious habit, I discovered how hard it was for me to stop shrugging my shoulders and present myself as the expert I'd worked so hard to become. As I worked on the shoulder shrug, I became comfortable with my voice of authority. As a result, I don't confuse my current audiences about whether I can be believed or not. Instead, I walk around, plant my feet, look squarely at the audience, and make my point with relaxed shoulders.

Toolkit for Making Your Walk Talk

Think of someone you know whose nonverbal behavior upsets you, or is in conflict with their verbal messages. First think of a question that asks for information about their nonverbal behavior. Then change the question by chalking it up to intuition. As an example, when someone you know scratches his neck, you may believe he's mad at you. In this instance, you might implement the following:

- *Nonverbal behavior question:* "When you scratch your neck, does that mean that you're annoyed with me?"

- *Intuition statement:* "I have the feeling you might be upset with me, and I want to check it out."

Now try writing down a question and a statement about non-verbal behavior that you'd like to ask someone in your life:

- *Your nonverbal behavior question:*
- *Your intuition statement:*

An Example of Making Your Walk Talk

Jason enjoyed going to lunch with Nate, a friendly rising star at his law firm. Unfortunately, Nate constantly looked at his watch during lunch. Jason figured that his co-worker thought he was boring and wanted to get back to the office, so he asked Nate this nonverbal behavior question: "I see you looking at your watch; are you enjoying your lunch?" Nate surprised him by replying, "It's not that; it's just that I have a new boss who's a stickler for punctuality, and when we have lunch I enjoy myself so much that I lose track of time." If Jason had continued to make assumptions about his co-worker's behavior, he might have lost a powerful ally.

The Voice of Authority

If our ears are tuned to the "voice channel," these voices will offer rich information. There are eight basic tones of voice or inflections. The "music" of each one is as different as jazz, rock, or soul. Each tone serves a purpose in communication, and getting the right *voice* is as important as the right words. The most common eight inflections people use are:

1. **Neutral:** This could be called the Dragnet tone, as it emphasizes facts: "She has brown hair." "It's the fourth house from the corner." "You're looking well."

2. **Commanding:** This voice expresses opinions and makes demands: "That was a terrific movie!" "Bedtime now!" "I need that report tomorrow!"

3. **Inquiring:** This voice turns the words into a question: "Are you hungry?" "Do you like the brochure?" "Do you want to go skiing?"

4. **Complaining:** This voice lets people know we're unhappy. Children use this voice extensively if they find that its grating quality gets their parents to cooperate. Adults also may find that whining works. Neutral words can be turned to complaints with a slight change in tone emphasizing certain words. Complaints can include both anger and sadness: "But I *don't* want to go to bed!" "I *really* want a cookie!" "I *should* get the promotion!"

5. **Angry:** This tone is easy to spot even when the person denies this emotion. Be aware that when people sound mad, they may actually be anxious: "Damn it!" "How could you?!" "I never get any breaks!"

6. **Affectionate:** This soothing voice lets people know that you care about them. It works best when you repeat back what others have said during communication because it conveys concern and empathy: "Of course you're worried." "I see you're upset that I'm late." "I really love you."

7. **Sad:** This tone can include disappointment, loss, or regret: "I wish I'd taken that job!" "I miss him!" "I'm so sorry!"

8. **Anxious:** This tone encompasses worry, concern, and fretting: "I'm going to run out of money!" "Did you lock the door?" "What if I have cancer?"

You've probably discovered how difficult it is to keep emotion out of your voice when you try to sound "rational." Our culture encourages people to use the neutral voice nearly all of the time, otherwise we may be thought of as immature. Tune in to any news program and really notice how odd it seems when the anchors use the neutral tone to inform you of horrible events such as "The Twin Towers have just been attacked by terrorists."

Particularly on the job, most folks believe that people should use their intellect and leave their emotions at home. When I conduct corporate-training seminars, I ask for a volunteer to demonstrate the silliness of expecting people to leave their feelings at home. I divide the room in two, labeling the left side "home" and the right side "workplace." Then I ask the volunteer to leave their emotions at home while they walk over to the workplace. As the volunteer arrives, I mischievously grin and ask if he or she accomplished the task. The volunteer and the rest of the group laugh at the silliness of my request and see that they bring their *whole selves* to work. If the comedy show *Saturday Night Live* wanted to do a spoof on workplace irrationality, they could call the sketch "Your Personality—You Can't Leave Home Without It!"

I've often had clients and readers of my syndicated column complain about co-workers who are acting too emotional. I ask them to reconsider their belief that rationality rules the world. If people's intellect dictated their lives, then we would have already dealt with world hunger and implemented world peace, and would have no more need for diet books. Our intellect doesn't run our lives because our emotions drive most decisions. Most of us can't implement what we *know* is "good for us" because we don't realize that our hearts are running the show.

We've formed a collective agreement that emotion is bad and intellect is good, so we often ignore body language or tones of voice that offer emotional information. Our intellect selects our words, but our emotions choose our body language and tone of voice. Most people communicate emotions in their voice without realizing it—for example, when you ask a friend, "What's the matter?" and she replies, "Nothing," in a sad voice. Or perhaps you ask a co-worker what he's mad about, and he barks back a loud "I'm fine!" The real message is carried not by the words but by the "music" in the voice. *(Are you still paying attention to your breathing?)*

When you use a tone of voice that doesn't correspond to your words, it's because your head disagrees with your heart. The following three conflicts will usually make you mismatch words and tone of voice:

1. *You know how you feel but think you shouldn't feel that way.* For example, you have a crush on someone at work, but one or both of you are married.

2. *You feel guilty about your feelings.* For example, you're mad because your mother calls too often, so the next time she calls and asks if you can talk, you say sarcastically, "Of course, Mom, I have all kinds of time to talk to you!"

3. *You're in denial about how you feel.* You're furious with your kids, but you believe good parents never hate their children. Thus, you may say loving words, but use an angry, harsh tone. Your children ask for a cookie and you're tired of saying no. You say sweetly, "Sure, why don't you eat the whole cookie jar," as you glare at them.

Some social questions use the tone of inquiry in a mismatched manner. An example of this is when people ask, "How are you?" but they don't use a sincere tone, and they don't care about your answer. Social rituals, however, aren't intended to confuse, but to be friendly *verbal grease.* (The handshake started as a way of making sure that the other person wasn't carrying a weapon, and of course we still shake hands today [even though most folks aren't carrying knives] to extend goodwill.) When people extend half-hearted invitations to lunch, or inquiries into your well-being, they don't *intend* to befuddle you. Of course, if someone repeatedly says "We must do lunch" with no interest in following through, then it's not unreasonable to ask for a specific time and date.

Often, the tone of inquiry is used in a confusing way to express anger, to indirectly ask for things, or to embarrass. For instance, false questions such as "Don't you have a more flattering suit?" are criticisms, not inquiries. Gender researchers have found that women are most likely to use such questions to indirectly express needs. For example, they may ask, "Are *you* hungry?" when *they* want to eat. If the person being questioned *isn't* hungry, the woman asking the question is now stuck with a no. If, instead, the woman said, "I'm hungry, and I'm going to fix a sandwich; do you want one?" she'd get better results.

If you ask for help indirectly, you run into the same problem. A question such as "Would you mind getting the mail?" only works if the other person thinks getting mail is a good idea. But a direct "I need your help picking up the mail" would be more effective. Some people use the tone of inquiry to humiliate others—for example, when asking an arrogant co-worker for an answer you know he doesn't have. But using inquiry to embarrass will only ensure that *you* have enemies. If you use questions when you aren't really curious, people will either be clueless about your needs or motivated to get even.

People often use a certain inflection without being aware of what tone they're using. When you have the Interpersonal Edge, you'll customarily pay attention to your tone, and choose the voice that will work best in your situation. The right tone in the right situation can work like magic. Let's practice being aware of the "soul" music in your tone of voice.

Toolkit for Developing a Voice of Authority

1. Set up a voice recorder by your phone at work and at home. Turn it on and then listen to the sound of your voice after a few calls. Which tone do you use the most? What do you notice about the volume, softness, and emotion in your voice as you speak? Do you sometimes use a tone that doesn't help your situation? Which inflection is the most comfortable or uncomfortable for you?

2. When you figure out which tone of voice is least comfortable for you, find opportunities to use it. (To review the eight voice inflections, see page 42.) For example, if you rarely use a commanding tone, tell your spouse or friend you need to practice it. Use it with them frequently until it becomes comfortable. To have the Interpersonal Edge, you need to be able to use all tones of voice well.

An Example of Developing the Voice of Authority

Marta put a voice recorder by her phone, and the next time her mother called she recorded their conversation. When she played it back, Marta was amazed to find out that when her mother asked for favors she didn't want to grant, she'd find herself agreeing, but her voice became soft and barely audible as she did so. The next time her mother called to ask for numerous favors, Marta also recorded the call and found that she used a clear, strong voice to say no to the help she didn't want to give. She discovered that she actually enjoyed her conversations with her mother for the first time in years when she used the voice of authority. *(Are you still paying attention to your breathing?)*

In the next chapter, we're going to journey into a surprising place to find your soul (right under your nose)—that is, your heart.

CHAPTER 4

THE HEART
OF THE MOMENT

"Your vision will become clear only when you can look into your own heart . . . . Who looks outside, dreams; who looks inside, awakes."

— Carl Jung

On tough days do you ever wonder who's controlling your life? You start a diet, set a work goal, or promise to break off that bad relationship, and poof!—nothing changes. The reason we often feel out of control is that our emotions drive our decisions, and for most of us, our heart is like an unknown and mysterious continent.

Who's Running Your Life?

One of my executive coaching clients, Janet, is a good example of how emotions exert powerful influence over behavior. She wanted to be promoted to senior manager but had one small problem. Yes, she was responsible, hardworking, and competent—until she fell apart crying in meetings. When she first came to me, I asked Janet what she was feeling when this happened. She said, "I have no idea. I'm fine, and then I'm sobbing."

Actually, Janet was feeling unappreciated, overworked, and unsupported but didn't notice these feelings until the emotional dam burst. We worked together so that she could recognize her physical and emotional clues that she was about to fall apart. With my help, Janet soon acknowledged, "When my stomach gets tight, my throat hurts, and my eyes burn, I need to leave before I lose it." I then taught Janet actions she could take at work so that her feelings didn't jam up in meetings.

Many people are like Janet. Without warning their emotions jump up, lock them in the trunk, and take off with their life. Before you can say mood swing, they've insulted a customer, told the boss she's an idiot, or exclaimed to a spouse that they never should have gotten married. Intellectual willpower has no effect on the strong currents that run our emotional life. Moreover, these currents, like ocean tides, can drown us if we refuse to acknowledge them.

These mood swings can also result in addictive and impulsive behavior. Binge eating, drinking, and other self-destructive habits take root in a heart that is unknown by the person whose body it's in. When we behave compulsively, others usually criticize us for our lack of discipline, and we also criticize ourselves. The reality is, if discipline actually worked, there wouldn't be so many weight-loss books on the bestseller list. It isn't like we don't know that we need to eat well and exercise. Each book promises that it has the magic cure for weight loss. The real magic cure (which isn't instant or easy) is to figure out what the heck is going on inside your heart. No amount of ice cream or alcohol can numb or fill a hungry heart. Anytime our behavior is compulsive or doesn't fit our intellectual goals, our heart has its own reasons.

One of my clients, Caroline, who'd been sexually abused by a family member, was predictably and painfully jumping from one bad relationship to the next. One day she started to speak in a voice that sounded like a small child. I asked her if she'd like to meet this child within. She reacted with a look of disdain and said, "She's a whiny wimp who wants to ruin my life. Why should I want to connect with her?" I told Caroline she might want to make this connection because the kid *was* going to ruin her life if she didn't.

As we worked together, Caroline understood the heart of her younger self. She cried and said with surprise, "She's not a bad kid . . . she's just so alone. She hasn't even had my support." That moment was the beginning of understanding the feelings that had driven Caroline into poor choices with men. In a short span of time, Caroline was engaged to a loving man and was excitedly planning her future.

If you want to live your life without having your emotions hijack your plans, you have to understand their power. This chapter follows the one on the magic of body language because your body is where you feel *(are you still aware of your breathing—hmm?)*. Most of us react to others in a knee-jerk fashion without knowing why certain situations upset us. Thus, we don't have the impulse control over our emotions in order to do what would work.

When my daughter was teething, my husband and I privately called her "Jaws" because she'd bite when she was mad. She took her adored blankie to playgroup, and the other kids decided that since she loved blankie, it must be pretty darn special, so they'd better nab it. She discovered that biting other children when they took her blankie fixed the problem quickly. She also got expelled from playgroup. We worked with her, saying, "We know you want to bite other kids when you're mad, but you just can't do it."

One summer day I picked up my little darling to give her the much-hated nap. She gave me a furious look and opened her mouth wide. I could tell she was *so* mad and wanted to chomp my bare shoulder *so* much. I told her that I knew she was angry and wanted to bite me. It was fine to be mad and fine to want to bite, but if she did, there would be no visit to the park later. She lunged with her mouth toward my shoulder and chomped air, then she sat back contentedly as I carried her toward her bed. I knew then that "Jaws" was gone, and my daughter was developing the ability to feel a strong emotion yet control her behavior. If I'd shamed her for wanting to bite or for being angry, she might have grown up to be one of those adults that *still* bite. Of course, adults bite with their *words,* but it still makes others bleed.

I tell clients in corporate seminars that the hardest part of using Social Sorcery tools won't be learning the intellectual knowledge, but instead will be identifying what they feel and then sitting with the feeling long enough to use what I'm teaching. For instance, to be able to ask questions about body language, you need to be able to "tolerate" not knowing everything. If you're too petrified to acknowledge that you aren't omniscient, even asking questions will be too uncomfortable.

Without information about our emotional reactions, we blame other people for our behavior. A parent can tell a child, "You made me hit you." A boss can tell an employee, "I yelled because you're not listening." A wife can tell a husband, "I cheated on you because you don't spend time with me." In reality, each person made a decision *influenced* by the other person but *independent* of that person. The parent, boss, and wife had many other choices. They chose to hit, yell, or cheat because of their own emotional reactions. If the wife took responsibility for her affair, she might say, "I felt lonely and wanted company and didn't want to risk asking you for intimacy anymore. I cheated on you because I was angry and wanted to hurt you." Other people affect us, but *we* alone make our choices.

Many books tell you to "be authentic" or "say what you feel" or "express your needs." These same books assume that everybody knows how to access this information. After over 26 years of working with people professionally, it's clear to me that most folks aren't walking emotional encyclopedias.

To be authentic or express your needs, you have to be able to articulately describe how you feel.

The Rainbow Soul: Naming Emotions

Emotions come in every color of the rainbow. And like a rainbow, there are just a few primary colors: *mad, sad, glad,* and *scared.* Most of us learn to identify colors in elementary school, but many of us never learn to correctly identify emotions. As I mentioned in an earlier chapter, in elementary school I wondered why we weren't taught how to get along. It was obvious to me that the kids (including me) didn't know how to deal with each other. As I grew up, I discovered that this lack of emotional education wasn't limited to the school-yard playground. I also realized that we often feel inadequate because we don't "naturally" know how to deal with other people well. We can then end up feeling uniquely flawed because we don't realize that we simply have an interpersonal-skill deficit, or a lack of education about emotions and people.

My corporate clients really struggle to identify feelings, since by convention, they're not authorized to have emotions at work. When I ask clients to identify what they're feeling, they usually make negative observations about others, such as "I'm feeling that Joe is undermining my work." If I point out that their comment is a thought and ask again about a feeling, they'll eventually pick a category like, "Okay, I'm mad."

It's often a breakthrough at work for people to even say they're mad. Being able to replace criticism about others with one simple emotional description about yourself such as "I'm mad" opens up a world of possibilities that can help fix the problem. By saying what you feel, you can more easily identify what you want and then suggest a solution that works for you. When my client is repeating, "Joe is undermining my work," neither Joe nor I have any idea what his co-worker wants.

Although we possess a wide range of emotional hues, we don't use the whole palette of color to express our reactions. When my daughter first learned to express anger, she used the word *hate* to express everything from how she felt about being furious to how she felt when it rained. One of her teachers told her that *hate* was a bad word. She came home and asked me about her teacher's comment. I said, "Honey, some people get nervous when you use the word *hate* because *hate* means "strong anger," and strong anger scares some folks. It's always okay to *feel* as if you hate someone or something. Any feeling you have inside is okay. It's all right to say you hate Mommy or Daddy or things at home. But it's not helpful to tell a friend you hate them because it hurts their feelings." I then came up with other words in the anger category, such as *annoyed, upset,* and *disappointed* that she could use to describe feeling mad to her teacher.

On an ongoing basis, my husband and I gave our daughter two messages to encourage her to recognize all her emotions:

1. There's nothing you can feel that's bad or wrong regard-less of what anybody else thinks.

2. There *are* "bad" choices that will generate consequences.

We felt that these messages were important to impart to our daughter because many kids get shamed as soon as they start ex-pressing emotions. The emotion doesn't go away; it gets denied. These children turn into adults who have smoke coming out their ears at the same time they claim they're not mad. Accepting the feelings of our children, ourselves, or other people can be uncom-fortable. It takes a bit of self-control when your child spits out "I hate you!" to respond with "You're really mad at me right now because I'm making you go to bed." Following up by giving your child a choice to go to bed now or lose their favorite toy makes it clear that any *feeling* is fine, but any behavior is not.

The Fickle Bluebird of Happiness

To validate a child's feelings while setting limits, it's neces-sary for parents to be able to tolerate it when their kids suffer. Many parents say, "I just want them to be happy" when asked what they want for their children. The problem is that the blue-bird of happiness is fickle. Constant happiness is both unachiev-able and unnecessary to have a good life. If the minute a child gets unhappy, parents step in, give in, or distract, the child then learns that happiness should be their North Star. Children who think that happiness is the benchmark of success end up avoiding important goals requiring temporary discomfort, sacrifice, or loss. Parents who believe that happiness is the benchmark of success won't let children's poor choices result in the necessary suffering that teaches them how to make wiser decisions.

A few weeks ago, my daughter refused to put on her shoes when it was time to leave for school. As always, whenever she makes a poor decision, as a consequence she then loses a favorite toy for the day. She was beside herself with grief and frustration about losing her beloved toy. As I watched her wallow in misery, I was aware of how much I love her and how painful it is for me when she suffers. I got down on her level, put my hand under her little chin, and said, "Honey, I know you're suffering and unhappy about the decision you made and about losing your toy. I'd like for you to be happy, but what I want *most* is for you to learn to make good decisions. You're probably going to suffer quite a bit as you learn to do that." I hugged her, and we drove to school.

When I was in my early 20s, my mother and I had repeated conversations about how much she wanted me to be "happy." During these chats I was puzzled by her definition of happiness. Did happiness mean not complaining, never being mad, or having to smile consistently? I also felt frustrated because many of my choices involved short-term discomfort with long-term benefits. My mother generously continued to engage in these conversations where I tried to explain my goals and she worried about my lack of constant bliss.

As I was experiencing a moment of hopelessness that I'd never convey my point, a new approach came to me. My mother had been raised Catholic and was still respectful of that tradition. I looked her squarely in the eye and said, "For heaven's sake, Mom, I'm glad you weren't the mother of Jesus, or Christianity would never have been invented!" She gave me a surprised look and stopped debating. I know that privately she still grieved my lack of perpetual happiness, but she no longer campaigned for me to share her unrealistic goal.

The Infection of Perfection

Most Western cultures treat emotions as if they need to be exorcised. The messages include: chill out, have a drink, smoke a cigarette, or take a day off. The goal is to present a happy, no-worries, neutral appearance at all times. One of my friends recently told me how people reacted when they found out that she was in therapy. She said, "Most people would have rather heard I was dieting and dropped 30 pounds than listen to the emotional baggage I was dropping."

There's a classic movie that was recently remade called *The Stepford Wives*. It's about a small New England town where the men secretly have their wives replaced with clone-like, perfectly pleasant robots who do everything the husbands want. Two sequels followed the original movie: *The Stepford Husbands* and *The Stepford Children*. In these films, the husbands or children were also murdered and replaced with perfect husbands and perfect children. These movies are all good metaphors, because it seems that the only way that people can constantly act perfectly agreeable is to kill off their inner life.

No human can be perfect, pleasant, or competent all the time. I have clients who admire people who *seem* perfect. We even tend to buy large quantities of *anything* from people who are good at projecting that illusion. Those who appear perfect make me nervous because I'm aware of the internal violence they've inflicted upon themselves in order to present this façade.

Social Sorcerers don't strive for seamless perfection. When you have the Interpersonal Edge, you won't fret about looking messy, awkward, or inadequate in the short run because you'll be more focused on long-term outcomes. Sometimes my clients come in wanting to use coaching or therapy to become flawless, but they're surprised to find that my advice is to let go of the infection of perfection to get what they want.

When we believe we need to struggle toward a "Stepford" image, we end up with a limited emotional vocabulary. We either say nothing about emotions, or we say we're *tired* or *stressed*. These labels aren't informative to other people.

Men struggle much more than women to be aware of or share emotional information. I tease my husband that women get more emotional support from their casual gym buddies than most guys get from their best friends. The sad part is that my humor contains an element of truth. Many of my male clients are bright, successful, ambitious guys, yet they all tell me how isolated they feel. They also think that they're unique and that *other* men have good friends and deep emotional connections. In my corporate communication classes when I ask the students to practice listening skills, I request that students choose topics with emotional content, and I ask the guys to select subjects other than sports. Many of the male students then laugh nervously and ask how to figure out what else they can talk about.

Few of us had parents or teachers who were able to teach us the subtle distinctions about how we felt (or how they felt). Instead of helping us match words to emotions, they were more likely to disregard any emotional content, saying "Pull yourself together," "Calm down," or "You're just hungry." You may even have been told that you weren't being yourself when you had strong feelings. When a little girl stomps her feet and starts yelling about a friend taking her toy, she's told that she's just tired. Then as adults, women wonder why they never get angry, but they sure do feel tired. A little boy may walk into the family room weeping about a friend who moved away only to be told that big boys don't cry. Then as adults, these same men wonder how to express all those feelings adult women seem to want them to have.

Feeling as a Foreign Language

When I do couples therapy or mediation in organizations, I often act as an "emotional thesaurus." That is, in couples therapy, I may ask a wife who's happily brimming over with tears to tell her husband how she feels. She merely says, "Good." I then suggest, "Do you think you feel relieved that he wants to work on the marriage? Do you feel *safe* and *surprised* that he's committed to you and *delighted* that he can express his strong feelings?" The wife often responds, "Yup."

Now I've got a rule that my clients can't point at me saying, "Yup, whatever she said." They at least have to repeat the message in their own words. I act like training wheels for my clients to help them develop an emotional vocabulary, but they have to be on the bike pushing the pedals. After working with me for a while, many couples make jokes when they're struggling to find words. I'll make some suggestions, then they'll point at me, and point at their spouse and mischievously ask, "Come on, can't I say 'what Skube said' this one time. I'm never gonna get this." I refuse to let them take the easy road and insist they keep doing the work. And, in short order, they discover their own emotional vocabulary.

When I'm doing mediation in a workplace, I also work as an interpreter. The way I rephrase my clients' language helps them stop fighting and work together productively. For instance, an upset boss I'm helping may start out by saying to an employee, "You're arrogant and uncooperative." I'll paraphrase what the boss said in a way that suggests a change in his language. For example, "So, are you saying that you're upset because there are behaviors you want from him that you haven't been able to get yet?" Usually the boss quickly agrees because he can see that his original language was counterproductive. He can also see that I've offered him a new language that's more likely to result in a resolution.

Toolkit for the Language of Feeling

If you're going to be an expert in any area, including emotions, you'll need to learn the vocabulary. For example, asking your boss whether he's "concerned" will probably work better than using the word "scared" since John Wayne and *real men* aren't suppose to be afraid. Being able to consciously choose the emotional intensity of words will let you paint your messages with the full spectrum of the emotional rainbow. You'll be able to speak powerfully, charismatically, and persuasively when you need to, and use muted tones when more neutrality (for example, in the midst of a heated conflict) is called for.

Check out the following palette of emotional colors. For each emotion, think about the primary feeling category you think that word belongs within: *sad, glad, scared,* or *mad.* (You might want to use a separate piece of paper to record your thoughts.) Notice that some words imply more than one emotion. Finally, in future conversations with your friends, family members, and co-workers, see how many of these colorful words you can integrate into your vocabulary.

As you look at the list of emotions, what's the difference in intensity between *irritated* and *furious?* Why do you use words like *disconcerted* when other times you'd just be *surprised?* Some words are also better suited for different environments. When you're proposing on bended knee, saying, "I'd find it interesting to see if you'd marry me," that probably sounds a little lukewarm. On the other hand, stating in a meeting with another company, "We're deliriously passionate about exploring a merger," is way too intense—unless it's a private meeting between two CEOs in love!

acrimonious	amazed	dismal	lonely	ambushed
lucky	angry	disturbed	melancholy	afraid
eager	offended	anxious	elated	optimistic
antagonistic	embittered	pathetic	apprehensive	electrified
pessimistic	blue	enthusiastic	petrified	attacked
enthralled	pitiful	astonished	enraptured	pleased
attracted	ecstatic	repelled	brave	excited
revolted	bold	exhilarated	sad	bored
fearful	scared	calm	fearless	shocked
cheerful	glad	shy	cautious	fortunate
sickened	captivated	frightened	sorrowful	content
stricken	startled	cheerless	grateful	stuck
confident	gratified	surprised	defeated	hateful
terrified	dejected	happy	timid	delirious
incredulous	trapped	disconsolate	hesitant	unhappy
despondent	jealous	unnerved	depressed	indisposed
worried	disconcerted	joyful	worthless	disgusted
jubilant	ashamed	guilty	grieving	repulsed

Okay, maybe during difficult moments, you often feel as if life is like a runaway train. Can you now see that taking charge of your life just involves having a little more emotional savvy? Once you start to understand the reasoning of the heart, you're ready for the next chapter, where you'll learn to be the CEO of "You, Inc."

CHAPTER 5

YOUR INNER CEO·

---

*"Advice is what we ask for when we
already know the answer but wish we didn't."*
— Erica Jong

As an executive coach, I've had the pleasure of working with highly talented CEOs, and I've found that the most effective leaders excel in getting various parts of the corporation to work together. They create peak performance because they listen carefully to all departments within the organization and integrate that information into wise and powerful choices.

You are, believe it or not, the CEO of "You, Inc." If you abdicate this position, then other people and random events will dictate your circumstances. If you want to take control of your life, you can't do it well without accessing information about yourself from all departments of your organization.

Running Your Life Like You're the Boss

The task of accessing full information about yourself may seem daunting, which may be the reason why so many of us still take those magazine tests promising instant insight into our personality. You may even be tempted to try the Psychic Friends Network to understand yourself better. Comedian Robin Williams once commented on the possibility that sources of answers outside of ourselves may be unreliable when he asked, "If it's the Psychic Network, why do they need a phone number?"

Overall, if you want to access your inner CEO, you'll need to learn how to truly listen to your body. By doing so, all your inner departments will be available to you.

The Body as a Soul Compass

First off, you can't figure out what you feel, or access your body's wisdom, by thinking. The word *feel* implies physical sensation. Even the word *emotion* has in its letters the implication that feeling is *e*-motion (that is, energy in motion—found in physical movement).

Our language demonstrates how physically disconnected we are. We'll say, "I've been suffering from this migraine," as if the pain in our head is the result of evil exterior forces. We'll complain about how our back goes out on us, as though our back muscles plotted mutiny. We describe our body symptoms as if they're a foreign force because, for many of us, our body is alien and mistrusted territory. We also use the word *it* frequently to describe our body. If asked about our headache, we might say, "*It* has been making *me* miserable for days," as if our head is a separate entity.

Disconnection from our body has a price. The anger we don't feel turns into a headache; the grief we can't express becomes a lump in our throat; the remorse over something we've done becomes a stomachache. On the other hand, if we identify and *own* these feelings, we can save ourselves a great deal of *dis-ease,* and at the same time become better communicators.

There are many books that talk about the connection between illness and disowned body feelings. There are also theories that state that illness is communication from our spirit to our mind about much-needed changes. Many of these books and theories are helpful because they make us think in new ways about what a powerful messenger of the soul the body can be. The downside of these theories presents itself if people decide they're to *blame* if they get sick. There's a big difference between *accountability* and *blame*. *Accountability* means you have the courage to explore all possible avenues to help yourself. *Blame* means that if you're still sick, you decide there's something inherently wrong with you.

It's one thing if you get cancer and wonder if there's information for you in the disease that could make you well (along with medical treatment). It's another thing if you explore this avenue, are still sick, and then decide you're bad or have failed.

In this chapter, I want to encourage you to become *accountable* and curious about your body, not to *blame* yourself for any pain or physical difficulties you experience. Blaming yourself or thinking you're bad always interferes with learning about yourself. If you're going to run "You, Inc.," well, you've got to have good-quality data.

No one I've ever met is so evolved that they can know exactly why things happen the way they do. If you're suffering from an illness, have explored all options, and are still sick—or worse, dying—it doesn't mean that you've failed. No one can prove that death is failure, and if you dig deep enough into the mystery and magic of your body, you'll become increasingly aware that death is not an end.

Sex, Lies, and Power

We often ignore our body except when we're being sexual. Even during exercise, we can engage in a routine that doesn't require us to fully feel it. When I teach nonverbal communication, I've been curious about how ashamed and uncomfortable my clients become even acknowledging their body movements. I've realized that our embarrassment about being physical affects our sex lives, our work lives, and our ability to understand ourselves.

The cultural lie is that the body is only identified with sensuality. The powerful truth is that your body contains a wealth of information about your *entire* life, not just your *sex* life. If you don't know what your body knows, you can suffer unnecessarily.

There's interesting religious mythology that encourages us to ignore our body, particularly if we aspire to be holy people. Imagine the conventional picture of the devil: cloven hooves, lower body of a goat, upper body of man, horns, and tail (in modern times he's been colored blood red). Many people don't realize that this image was originally Pan, a god of Greek mythology. However, Pan was associated with sensuality and the earth, and was a protector of wild things. He played the flute, lived a merry life in the woods, and occasionally chased after wood nymphs. There was nothing inherently evil in the Greek myths surrounding Pan.

You might wonder why Pan was chosen to represent the devil. Is there something in modern religions that distrusts the physical? If in reality, the body is the portal through which we can contact our heart and soul, then what effect does all this mistrust have on people who are trying to evolve spiritually? If diving deeply into the physical self is discouraged, then where else can we find such a reliable compass for direct contact with Spirit? And you really have to wonder, if the body is the compass of the soul, who's behind the whole "body is evil" campaign?

The next two exercises will introduce you to the wisdom waiting inside of you, as I'll describe how to scan your body for emotional information. You can also tape-record these directions, then close your eyes and listen to the exercise on tape. The first scan will help you identify habitually tense and loose areas. The second scan will focus your awareness on what the sensations tell you about your feelings.

Toolkit for Sex, Lies, and Power

Basic body scan: The body scan isn't a relaxation exercise, so don't feel that you have to ease any uncomfortable feelings or sensations you discover. When you get done, you may feel more relaxed, but if you feel more agitated or uncomfortable, that's also fine.

Put yourself in a comfortable, quiet position, but make sure your head isn't supported or you might fall asleep. Close your eyes and focus on your breathing. Slowly, starting with your head, mentally go through your body and notice any tension, loose places, or pain. Move through your jaws . . . eyes . . . ears . . . tongue . . . and into your neck. Mentally scan your neck . . . back . . . and rib cage. Keep focusing on breathing deeply and slowly. Notice your chest . . . stomach . . . internal organs . . . shoulders . . . arms . . . and hands. Now move into your hips . . . buttocks . . . and into your legs.

Last, mentally scan your ankles . . . feet . . . toes . . . and soles of your feet. Now relax and continue to breathe slowly and deeply as you allow yourself to sink into your body even further. Take a deep breath and focus on each of the areas of discomfort or sensation you become aware of during your body scan. Allow yourself to notice the sensations in your body without changing anything. Notice what it's like to take the time to completely feel your body. At your own pace, as you're ready, slowly open your eyes.

Now take a pencil and mark on the following unisex figures any spot that was tense or painful. Use the letter "T" for tension and the letter "P" for pain. Next to the "T" or the "P" use a dash (—) if the tension or pain was intermittent, and use a plus sign (+) if it was continuous. You can also get playful with crayons and use different colors to describe the distinctive sensations in your body. Your stomach might be colored red for burning, and your throat might be colored blue because it feels cool.

With this initial scan, you'll get an idea of where you're tense, loose, in pain, or comfortable in your body. The first time you do it, don't be surprised if you feel numb. It may take a few sessions before you realize, for example, that your upper back aches. There's no right way to do body scans, and there's no way to fail—you can't fail to increase your awareness. Anything you discover, including numbness, increases your understanding of your body.

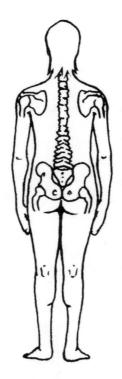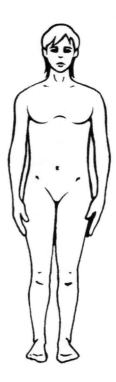

Advanced body scan: The wisdom and language of the body is typically a faint, quiet voice. When the body does scream with an intense backache, migraine, or a serious illness, we usually don't understand the communication. The advanced body scan will introduce you to your "bodyspeak." We're going to amplify any of the pain or tension you felt in the basic scan. The reason I'm asking you to amplify the discomfort is not because I'd like to see you suffer; I'm asking you to increase the volume on your body's *voice* so you can hear what your body is *saying*.

Get yourself in a comfortable position again, with closed eyes and your head unsupported. Be aware that the advanced body scan is a powerful exercise that can put you in touch with strong feelings, so breathing deeply and consistently is critical. A good supply of oxygen will help you *feel* more fully. You'll also be less likely to leave this exercise with a head- or stomachache. Choose a place on your body that you labeled tense in the basic body scan. Put your entire attention on this discomfort and try to make it worse. If it burns, try to make the burn hotter. If it's tight, try to make the constriction tighter. Keep working to make it worse. Imagine that you're filling the whole room with this tension, then the whole house, and then the whole city. Keep breathing deeply as you do so.

As the sensation becomes more painful, notice whether it has a color, a shape, or makes any noise. Don't be surprised if you get weird images like a hammer, a knot, or a fist. Also don't be surprised if you find yourself contorted into a strange position as you make the sensation worse. Your back may arch, you may scrunch your shoulders, or puff out your chest as you exaggerate tense areas of your body. Keep breathing. As you focus on the pain, notice if part of you wants to ignore it or make it go away. Notice whether the pain feels like sadness, anger, or fear. If the tension becomes too much and there's a strong emotion underneath, you may find yourself spacing out or going numb. If you feel like the exercise is becoming emotionally overwhelming, it's fine to stop and come back later. Our body has circuit breakers that kick in when too much energy or consciousness is flowing through our system. If you feel anesthetized, simply open your eyes, let your body reset the circuit, and try it later.

As you continue to focus on the tension, allow yourself to remember a time in your life when you've felt this pain before. Don't worry if your mind doesn't seem to know—your body does. Be curious and let any memories play as though they were pictures in a slide show. If you don't get memories immediately, that's okay. Just keep breathing, being curious, and making the sensations worse. Notice the emotions connected with the physical sensation or the memories. You may have many memories and emotions coming up, or your attention may be on one incident.

People get memories in different ways. Some people see pictures, and some feel the sensations in their body. Any way that you remember is fine. If you're focused on one memory, ask yourself what you wished you could have said or done differently. If you're focused on several, wonder about the themes. Are you seeing scenarios where people treated you badly and you couldn't protect yourself? Are you seeing moments where you were frightened and couldn't ask for help? The discomfort in your body will help you understand something about emotions that are difficult and memories where these emotions were invoked. Keep breathing deeply. Allow yourself to explore this place in any way that feels helpful to you, and when you're ready, take a deep breath and open your eyes.

Repeat this process for as many tense places as you wish. You'll become more aware of the emotions your body holds as you review this process. A side benefit is that you'll relax those chronically tense places. People are often surprised to find that when they try to relax a muscle, it gets worse; and when they tense the muscle, it relaxes. Most relaxation exercises even use the process of tensing muscles to achieve their goal. As you become consciously aware of the emotions your body is holding, these feelings (and the tension) start to release. If you become overwhelmed with emotions that feel too frightening or painful to work on by yourself, seek out the services of a counselor. Our culture overemphasizes independence and makes people feel ashamed to ask for assistance. Why not get help to release the chronic tension you've been carrying around, rather than continue to suffer because you're worried about asking for help?

An Example of Sex, Lies, and Power

When I was writing my dissertation and working full-time, my back developed a spasm so painful that it confined me to my bed. As I was lying there, I went into the pain and tried to make it worse so that I could "turn up the volume" on the message within the discomfort. My back felt achy and tired. As I focused on increasing the sensations, I began to notice how frustrated I felt that I was working all the time. I heard the words *Back off!* echoing in my head, and realized that I couldn't remember the last time I'd done something fun. I opened my eyes, rolled over carefully, picked up the phone, and scheduled a vacation. As I got off the phone, I realized that my back pain was gone.

Now vacations aren't always the answer, and this was an unusually fast physical response (I'm not always this lucky), but it does emphasize how much the body knows. Our minds often think we're limitless, but our body reminds us to slow down and tells us what we need to revitalize ourselves.

I suggest that you practice the basic and advanced body-scan techniques several times a week until it becomes easier to notice discomfort in your body, what you're feeling, and what you'd like to have happen. Then you'll begin to observe emotional patterns that come up in different situations. For instance, let's say that every time someone in authority asks you to do something, you feel resentful, afraid, and forced to comply. As you work with the body scans and release the anger and fear, you'll be able to ask questions, set better limits (even with authority figures), and realize that you always have a choice to comply or not.

The Enlightenment Snooze Button

Last week my yoga teacher was getting the class ready to meditate. He talked about the emotional discomfort that can come up when we contact our inner selves. He then challenged the class, "If you're not going to get enlightened now, then when?" Most of my fellow students tended to contemplate rather than respond to his questions. But I took him up on that query and said, "I've heard every answer imaginable: 'It's too hard, I don't have the time, a vacation will work better,' and 'I'm too scared.' Do you need any more answers?" The class chuckled because we all know how tempting it is to hit the snooze button on enlightenment.

Unfortunately, higher awareness has never had an effective global public-relations campaign. We can always point to Jesus as an example of why enlightenment can be a bad idea. Don't get me wrong—he was a great teacher, but the price Jesus paid was pretty steep—being nailed to a cross by doubters and disbelievers. I've always wondered whose side has been promoting that whole martyrdom thing. I figure either we've misunderstood the point of the story, or the devil's got a really good public-relations staff.

Now Buddha seemed to come through the whole experience unscathed, but maybe he was a fluke, because we have all the religious martyrs. I've always been fond of Joan of Arc, who supposedly talked directly to angels, but Joan's enlightenment price tag was similar to Jesus'. So, for the "average bear," enlightenment begins to look like pretty hard work with dubious results. Most of us probably figure, "Hey, it's going to be hard to put me on a cross or burn me at the stake if I'm safe, cozy, and unconscious in bed."

Throughout recorded history, enlightenment has never been "for everybody." Recently, one of my coaching clients, Jonathan, was contemplating getting into therapy because he had some deep underlying issues. He was a bright, ambitious guy who'd been sent to me because he was driving his CEO crazy. After we worked together for a few sessions, Jonathan was able to stop many of the behaviors that were undermining his career. He could also see that he didn't have the insight or ability to stop engaging in other negative behaviors, even though he now intellectually understood that they were impeding his advancement.

As we finished the coaching, we discussed whether therapy would be useful. "Dr. Skube," Jonathan asked in a charming voice, "aren't there some small tools you can give me to fix these other problems?" I explained to him that if I wanted to make money, I could lie to him. I told Jonathan that I'd already given him all the tools he could use intellectually. Sometimes these tools work, but sometimes the problem isn't with the head but the heart. I told him that I've seen people who read books, listen to tapes, and take weekend seminars that are focused on intellectual answers. They then figure that they must be unfixable because their troubles persist.

I told Jonathan that when a problem can't be fixed intellectually, it's like a broken arm that has healed improperly. I can put lots of cute cartoon Band-Aids on the arm, but it still won't function well. If there were a way around rebreaking a bone and resetting it, I'd use it on my own wounds. I finished by stating that the work of rebreaking the bone and resetting it is too hard to embark upon lightly.

Many of us find ourselves at the same crossroads as Jonathan. Do we try to fix our lives with Band-Aids, or do we tackle the underlying problems? Now there's nothing inherently wrong with vacations, a glass of wine, or other occasional breaks from the stress of life. Nobody I know could handle full awareness of themselves 24 hours a day. However, when we *habitually* use distractions to avoid our deeper selves, we often end up making choices that create intense, long-term pain. We get diabetes from overeating, get divorced from repeated "fun" affairs, or find ourselves in financial ruin as a result of lavish spending.

Buddha, being very observant, noticed right off the bat that life is suffering. He pointed out that you could distract yourself all you want and at the end of the day your suffering will still be there. He strongly suggested that trying to avoid suffering actually generated *more* suffering. Many people still don't get that one. They just figure that Buddha was more of a pessimist than a realist.

When corporate or private clients come to me in great pain, I tell them that they're *lucky,* because I've found that people who are hurting are more motivated to make changes. When clients come to me who are merely mildly uncomfortable, they're more tempted to hit the snooze button. They often have to go back out and keep on with what they're doing until they're in great pain. Only then will they be willing to learn a better way.

Life is a lot like my earlier body scans because when we're trying to ignore tension in our body or our life, it tends to get worse. When we acknowledge the pain, we can then be open to a course of action to create a solution. If there's no solution, then we can let go because the problem isn't within our control. If you relax in the face of suffering, you won't necessarily become happy all the time, but you will experience a new underlying sense of peace when you don't struggle against the circumstances in life that you cannot control or change.

People have complained to me that when they postpone dealing with their emotional issues, they feel like sleepwalking zombies. The upside to being a zombie is that you may end up in a deep rut (sometimes called a grave), but you usually avoid crosses. Unfortunately, being a zombie can feel a lot like a cross of a different sort. Our overindulgent culture encourages a fog of numbness that can make us forget who we are. When you know how to listen to your body to find out what you feel, what you want, and who you are, you'll have the information you need to effectively run your life. Your body will be a *soul compass* that may guide you in different ways than others go, but it will always guide you in the direction of your own true north.

As you listen deeply to your own body, you'll come to easily understand the motivations, feelings, and agendas of other people you work with and love. When you aren't distracted, disturbed, or distressed by what's going on within yourself, other people will be easier to understand and influence.

PART II

IMPROVING EFFECTIVENESS WITH OTHERS

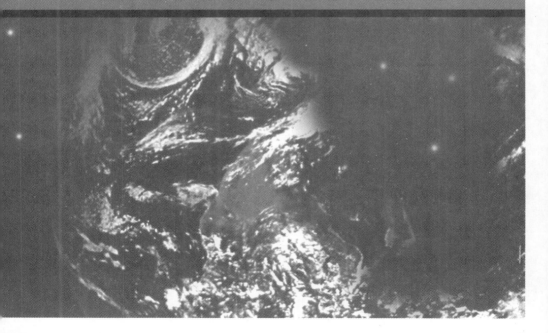

CHAPTER 6

EVERYONE IS YOUR CUSTOMER, SO LISTEN

"The greatest compliment that was ever paid me was when one asked what I thought, and attended to my answer."
— Henry David Thoreau

When you want your mate to go to the movies with you, expect your kids to clean their rooms, and hope that your employees will be motivated, do you think you'll persuade them via brilliant arguments? Well, you won't. Everyone in your life is actually a customer who has personal or professional business to transact with you, so if you know how to listen, your words will target the emotional bull's-eye in your "customer." If you figure that talking *more* will do the trick, you'll simply be filling up the airwaves with words that don't influence, persuade, or motivate.

The Business of Listening

The biggest myth about listening is that just because we have two ears, we're able to hear what others say. The reality is that our own preconceptions, emotional reactions, and agendas interfere with hearing. We typically assume in a conversation that we're both talking about the same thing. Imagine instead that there's a force field around you and every person with whom you interact. Now imagine that the words people hear are warped or distorted when they enter this invisible field. Can you now see how complicated it is to straighten out words and hear without distortion? The following illustration shows examples of how messages get warped and outlines the common reasons why people distort the words of others:

PERSON A Message Sent	**PERSON B** Message Heard Through Warp Field
Did you get that report done?	He thinks I'm lazy
Did you recheck those numbers?	She thinks I'm stupid
Would you like to go to lunch?	He wants to manipulate me!
Have a good day!	She wants to tell me how to be
Did you remember to get milk?	He's trying to control me
I love you!	She wants to ask for something
Good job!	He wants me to work overtime
Why did you want to talk?	She's angry and setting me up

1. *Different interpretations of words:* "The word *love* means never saying you're sorry."

2. *Words or phrases that remind you of painful childhood relationships:* "She's just as critical and controlling as my mother!"

3. *Jumping to conclusions:* "I know what you're saying, but you're wrong."

4. *Assumptions:* "Yeah, I know, you're going to boss me around like you always do."

5. *Getting defensive:* "I don't have to listen to this kind of crap!"

We tend to do a million things rather than listening. The following list covers some of the popular distractions that keep us from being good listeners:

- Thinking up our next response
- Having difficulty concentrating
- Holding preconceived ideas
- Being bored
- Daydreaming
- Arguing with the speaker in our head while someone's talking
- Listening only for facts (ignoring emotional content)
- Wanting to be right
- Watching our surroundings rather than the speaker

I'll bet you could identify a few habits on this list that you've indulged in while you appeared to be listening. Giving a speaker your full attention is tough, because people think at a rate of over 400 words per minute, but speakers can rarely talk faster than 175 words per minute. During the time lag between speaking and thinking, we don't know what to do. Obviously, if we want to hear not just the words but the soul of a communication, we need simple tools to help us get what others are really saying.

Basic Ears: Paraphrasing

Since we think much faster than people speak, it's natural to drift into our thoughts. The easiest way to stop the distortions and pay attention during communication is by paraphrasing, which is what I call "Basic Ears," where you verbally repeat in your own words what you just heard. When you know that you have to remember what the speaker just said, you pay closer attention. Moreover, by repeating the content to the speaker in your own words, you'll often grasp new meaning. One of my clients, Katrina, says that paraphrasing is like listening twice: once with your ears, internally; and the second time with your words, externally.

When people confuse the message received with the one that's intended, communication turns into a bad science-fiction movie where invisible warp fields control people's minds. When we repeat back what we heard, the emotional warp field becomes visible and can be deactivated. When we use Basic Ears, we assume that distortions are going to happen. We don't take action on our assumptions about what we heard before we check it out (which often saves us from looking foolish or alienating others).

For instance, when I write my advice column, I only have space for 450 words to answer two often-complex questions. Sometimes I'll get an angry letter from a reader who feels offended that I left out some pertinent information. For example, I recently wrote a column about how some people tend to get depressed in the winter. I recommended that these people should first get a medical evaluation to rule out physical causes, and I then went on to talk about some of the emotional reasons why people get depressed. I was surprised when five readers wrote me letters saying that they were upset that I didn't discuss Seasonal Affect Disorder (SAD), which is a physical condition related to light deficiency. Each of these individuals assumed that I was unaware of this condition, or had irresponsibly left it out of my response. In fact, I simply didn't have enough column space to cover every possible contingency.

When we make negative assumptions, other people won't want to do what we desire because they feel unjustly accused. Instead of outright assuming I was being incompetent or irresponsible, those five readers could have paraphrased and inquired, "Dr. Skube when you recommended that people rule out a physical condition, did you put SAD in that category? I'd like to know more about SAD." I would have then been motivated to offer detailed information about SAD in a future column.

It's easy to get huffy when we believe that a person has done us wrong. It's not the norm (but useful) to slow down and ask questions before we assume that the other person intended to harm us. People are more likely to help you if you're not jumping to the conclusion that they're out to get you.

Now when you paraphrase, it's best to use synonyms rather than the exact words; otherwise, you might get called "Polly" and handed a cracker! For example, if a customer tells you he's angry, you could use the word *upset* or *irritated* rather than the word *angry* in your paraphrase. The only time you want to use the exact words is when a pet phrase is involved. For instance, if your boss frequently says, "Can you think of something that would 'wow' the clients?," you'd want to use the word *wow* in the paraphrase, saying, "I think this brochure has the 'wow' factor because of the intense graphics!" since it's the *exact* term your boss likes to utter.

You'll learn a well-kept secret if you paraphrase: Most people don't listen to themselves when they talk, so when you repeat their message, it's usually the first time they've heard it. When you paraphrase, people become aware of what they're saying. If they're trying to mess with you, it will be hard for them to deny what they've said. When you repeat back the communications of those who are being straightforward with you, they'll often regard you as brilliant, insightful, and trustworthy, because people often mention solutions to problems as they chat. When you repeat back what they've said, they'll be in awe of *your* great solutions.

To paraphrase effectively, start each sentence with a tag phrase that tells the listener you're asking a question. Good tag phrases include:

- "Let me see if I understand you correctly . . ."
- "So you're saying . . ."
- "If I understand what you're saying . . ."

If you neglect to use a tag phrase, it will sound like you're telling people what they think. Since most of us don't want to make anyone hostile, I recommend that you try to remember the tag phrase. In practicing paraphrasing, you also might typically make the following blunders:

1. Feeling like you have a neon sign flashing on your head that says, "I'm now paraphrasing you," and worrying that others will get mad. People are so hungry to be heard that they usually won't notice that you're practicing a new technique. They will, however, feel more understood.

2. Forgetting that paraphrasing means that you don't respond out loud with your own ideas to what someone has said. If you notice yourself responding instead of paraphrasing, imagine that you're sitting by someone who's hard of hearing who asks you to repeat back what you heard. You can also imagine that you're like a mirror reflecting back the other person's message.

3. Waiting too long to paraphrase because you're afraid to interrupt, and then you can't remember what was said. Use your hands and eyes to interrupt so you can paraphrase. You can say, "Wait a minute" or "Excuse me," while motioning with your hands to capture the attention of the speaker.

4. Repeating back what you heard, but with a tone of voice or body language that's hostile or accusing. Make sure you're as neutral as possible. If you're angry for some reason, it's better to tell the other person you need time to think. Take a minute or more to cool off before you resume. If you've done the nonverbal exercises in the Divine Body chapter, you'll have a good idea how you sound in the neutral voice, and how you look when using neutral body language.

5. Paraphrasing indiscriminately. This isn't a tool to be used at the grocery store when the checker asks if you want paper or plastic. The best times to use it include: clarifying directions, creating trust, working through conflicts, understanding differences, creating rapport, or buying time so you can think of an appropriate response.

6. Believing that if you paraphrase when people are upset, they'll automatically respond pleasantly and immediately cooperate. In reality, during conflicts, people frequently get angrier or more emotional when they're paraphrased. The trick is to keep paraphrasing until the other person has finished venting. At the end of the paraphrase, ask, "Is there anything else?" When other people have emptied out *their* thoughts and feelings, they'll be ready to receive *your* thoughts and feelings with less distortions, warped reactions, or defensiveness.

7. Forgetting that paraphrasing is not agreement. Paraphrasing is the demonstration of understanding. You can vehemently disagree and still paraphrase in a neutral way. It just takes practice.

8. Worrying about being accurate. It's okay to be wrong when you paraphrase. The other person then has a chance to correct your perception. Also, there will be times that you're right, but the person argues with your paraphrase. In this case, you can simply shrug and say, "Well, then, what are you saying? I'm confused."

Toolkit for Basic Ears (Written Practice)

Read the example and then paraphrase the statements that follow. Make sure you add the pronoun "you" as you paraphrase. For example, rather than saying, "It sounds like I'm a jerk," you would say, "It sounds like *you* think I'm a jerk." This clarifies that it's the opinion of the other person. Remember to use tag sentences to indicate that you're asking a question. For example:

Statement: "If you weren't so critical of my work, I'd be able to get more done and I wouldn't be late so often."

Paraphrase: So are you saying that my criticism of your work is causing you to be less productive and preventing you from getting to work on time?"

Now you try:
Statement: "You always let details fall through the cracks, and now we're probably going to lose this client because you and your department didn't follow through."
Your Paraphrase:

Statement: "Well, if you can't help get the house cleaned up, I don't think I'll have time to go to your business function tonight!"
Your Paraphrase:

Statement: "Thanks for staying overtime every night this week. I don't think we would have met the deadline without your working so hard to make it happen."
Your Paraphrase:

Getting good at paraphrasing takes practice. Many Social Sorcery techniques are like martial-arts movements. If you don't test them out in easy situations, you won't be able to perform effectively when you really need the technique. You've probably heard that the three rules of real estate success are: location, location, and location. The three rules of developing the Interpersonal Edge are: practice, practice, and practice.

In my classes and in the exercises in this book, I include a compliment in my paraphrasing examples because it makes people realize how they habitually react to them. When we get a compliment, we often freeze up, and worry about appearing smug or looking arrogant. Often we even feel uncomfortable saying "Thank you," so there's no way we'd consider paraphrasing a compliment. But the reason why you *should* paraphrase, especially nice remarks is that when you paraphrase praise, you acknowledge a gift that people are taking the trouble to give you. And you'll encourage them to pay you more compliments in the future.

For example, let's say you wrote a thank-you letter to a teacher who changed your life. It might read: "I want you to know how important your classes were, and that my life has been permanently improved. I'm profoundly grateful to you!" You probably wouldn't be upset if he or she simply replied, "Thank you." However, you probably would feel more acknowledged if this person wrote back and said, "It sounds like my classes made a huge difference in your life and you really wanted me to know how helpful it has been to you."

For the most part, it's our own egos that get in the way of acknowledging other people. Ironically, the same thing that keeps us from paraphrasing a compliment can also keep us from paraphrasing an insult—we don't want to look bad.

Toolkit for Basic Ears (Live Practice)

Paraphrasing on paper is challenging enough, but doing so in the real world, in real time, can be tough the first few times you try it, so be patient with yourself. Realize that you're building new habits, and that most of us don't listen to others even when we think we do. Also be aware that many of us, as adults, stop trying or learning new things. Moreover, give yourself a big pat on the back because you've got the courage and willingness to learn something new that may feel awkward at first.

- **Level 1:** Tell three friends or co-workers that you're practicing paraphrasing. Ask if they'd be willing to help you. Suggest that they talk about something important to them as you paraphrase for five minutes. Make sure that you don't start responding, giving them advice, or telling them what you think. Get feedback from them about how you're doing and how they're reacting to the technique. Ask them to tell you specifically what you missed when you paraphrased them.

- **Level 2:** Pick three people you don't know well, and during a conversation with them try paraphrasing. Be sure to ask them, "Is there anything else?" or "Is that right?" to get valuable information.

- **Level 3:** Next time you find yourself in an argument, use paraphrasing and get feedback.

An Example of Basic Ears (Live Practice)

Karen was having an argument with her husband, Michael, about whether or not they could afford a vacation. Instead of engaging in her usual behavior and telling him why he was wrong, she paraphrased his words, saying, "So Michael, it sounds like you're really worried about money." He looked surprised, stopped telling her she was being selfish, and said, "I just don't know if we can start a family this year and also take this cruise."

Now it was Karen's turn to be surprised. It turned out that Michael thought she wanted to have their first baby this year and was worried about setting money aside. She told him that she didn't want to get pregnant this year, and they happily planned a romantic cruise with no worries and no fights.

Advanced Ears: Emotions and Hidden Agendas

Once you've got Basic Ears down, you can proceed to a sometimes-magical technique I call "amplification" or Advanced Ears. In the beginning, I want my students to focus on the words of the speaker. However, as my students become more advanced, I ask them to listen for emotion in a communication. At the core of every message is a feeling surrounded by words:

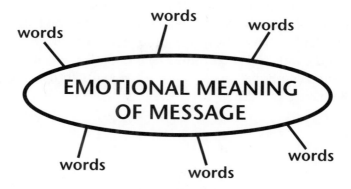

In Basic Ears, it's possible to technically repeat words but fail to grasp the *soul* of the message. In order to influence people, you must understand the emotional content of their communication.

I remember listening to my friend Carrie talk about how everything in her life was going well as we were planning a trip. As she talked, her voice sounded worried and her face looked concerned. She also seemed reluctant to commit to the trip.

To acknowledge Carrie's anxiety, I paraphrased, "So it sounds like everything in your life is going really well, yet you're still worried?" I ended my paraphrase in a question mark to emphasize that I was making an inquiry, not a statement. My friend then talked about how nervous she got when things went smoothly. Being able to take a nice trip was making her more nervous because she was waiting for the other shoe to drop. After talking to me about her anxiety, Carrie committed to the trip because she saw why she was hesitating. She joked that since the pleasure police weren't going to take her away, she might as well enjoy the trip.

Amplification can even clear up emotional distortions that occur when you listen to other people's relationships. For example, I was having lunch with married friends of mine when the husband, Sam, told his wife, Barb, that she shouldn't order red wine because it would make her nose stuffy. Barb asked Sam where he heard that information. He got angry and I asked him why. He told me, "Barb thinks I'm stupid and never believes me." Barb was surprised and said that she questions him because she has trouble trusting people and needs some background information.

If Sam had simply *amplified* his wife's question and said, "I heard you ask me how I know about the red wine, and I also heard that you don't believe I know what I'm talking about," Barb could have then cleared up the misunderstanding. If the couple didn't realize their emotional distortions, they would start fighting every time Barb questioned him.

Toolkit for Advanced Ears

In Basic Ears, the focus is on the words. In Advanced Ears, the speaker's emotion is the focus. Read the following sentences, and write an *amplification* statement that paraphrases the underlying feeling:

Example: "I hate it when you're always looking over my shoulder when I'm trying to finish a report."

Paraphrase: "Let me see if I understand you: You get angry at me when you feel that I don't trust you to get your work done, and you feel pressured when I check in on your progress. Is there anything else?"

Statement: "You expect me to know what you want, but you don't tell me, and then you blame me for not doing the right thing."

Your Paraphrase:

Statement: "If other people in the office ask you for help, you help them. But when *I* ask for help, you're too busy, and I have to remind you a million times."

Your Paraphrase:

Statement: "Have you been taking some psychobabble classes? Why are you repeating what I said? Do you think I'm deaf and don't know what I said?!"

Your Paraphrase:

An Example of Advanced Ears

Patty paused as her customer, John, said for the third time, "You sell crappy computers; I'm on deadline and you have some stupid policy I'm supposed to care about?!" The first two times, Patty had been busy explaining policy to the customer. This time, Patty took a deep breath and said, "John, it sounds like you're really annoyed, the computer we sold you isn't working, and you've got to get a project finished by tomorrow."

Smoke ceased to pour from John's ears as he simply agreed. Patty now understood the problem, found a solution that fit company policy, and allowed John to meet his deadlines. John went on to write a glowing letter of appreciation to Patty's immediate supervisor, her regional manager, and the CEO. Based on her advanced listening to John and other customers that followed him, Patty ended up with the top bonus of any salesperson that year.

If people get mad when you amplify or paraphrase their message, here are the magic words to calm them down: "I've learned that I don't listen well sometimes, and I really want to understand what you're saying. This is the only way I know how to check out if what I heard is what you meant." No one who knows you will disagree that sometimes you don't listen well. I've also never had someone jump up and exclaim, "No! No! Don't do that—I hate it when someone tries to understand me!" Once people understand that your intention is to understand them, they'll settle down unless:

1. They have other emotional issues with you.
2. They're trying to hide their own agenda.

If people have issues with you, like they feel you're always trying to control them, are criticizing them, or are being condescending, the magic words probably won't work. Surprisingly, what works best then is to simply paraphrase their issues, such as: "So you believe I'm repeating your words to try to control you?" If you keep paraphrasing, they'll feel that you know what they want, and the conflict will be clarified if not resolved. If your intention, of course, *is* to control, criticize, or embarrass, no amount of explanation will clear up the situation. You're better off admitting that you're upset and waiting until you cool off to talk.

If people are hiding their agendas, you'll make it impossible for them to mess with you if you use amplification because the real issues will become clear. Social Sorcerers, on the other hand, don't volunteer to be messed with. With agenda hiders, you want to keep paraphrasing (think *Columbo*-style) until they see that you're onto them. Don't bother trying to argue, make statements, or defend yourself. You'll be highly effective if you keep repeating their meaning back to them while they deny what you understood. When you leave the conversation, it's fine to claim confusion. You still have made it clear you won't play the hidden-agenda game.

Now that you know how to listen to all the *customers* in your life, you might be curious how to get them to *want* to listen to you. The next chapter will show you how to avoid being misunderstood and teach you how to shift people's perceptions of you.

CHAPTER 7

GETTING PEOPLE TO LISTEN TO YOU

*"I know you believe you understand what you think I said, but
I am not sure you realize that what you heard is not what I meant."*

— Anonymous

As you become a good listener, you'll begin to hear information that others aren't admitting or even aware of. If you try
to repeat back these denied statements, people may do a fright-
ened-porcupine imitation and start throwing quills. Sometimes
you might be wrong about what you heard, but that's the point of
paraphrasing. Go back and ask the speaker to continue providing
information so that you can clarify the message.

If the person is becoming uncomfortable as you paraphrase,
don't try to nail them on admitting the truth. You'll know that
you've learned something valuable that the speaker isn't ready to
digest. Your new information will help you connect with and influence the person. Just murmur something that lets them off the

hook like, "Well, I might not understand what you're saying," or "This might not be the best time to talk." Make it clear that you're open to resuming the conversation whenever they want.

Lord, Don't Let Me Be Misunderstood

As you see how well your listening skills are working, you'll also be eager to ask others to paraphrase *you*. If you're having a conflict, giving directions, or are unsure how your words are being interpreted, simply ask to have your words repeated back. It's important to avoid giving the impression that you think the other person is slow witted. You can say, "I'm not sure I'm being clear. Can you tell me what you're hearing?" or "What are you hearing me say?" These words let people know that you're asking for help, not criticizing their listening skills.

For example, in an executive-coaching session, I was trying to tell my client Brad how he could have handled a performance appraisal more effectively. The more we talked, the more tense he became. I finally stopped and asked him, "What are you hearing me say?" He burst out, "I think you believe I really blew this appraisal, and I don't think you appreciate that I've improved the way I work with this employee."

I asked Brad to expand on his thoughts about my *perceived* criticism and listened. I then told him I believed he'd done a great job. I specifically acknowledged the ways in which he'd improved his communication skills. I added that since he wanted to learn ways to motivate this employee, he'd asked me to point out options. Because I took the time to ask Brad what he was hearing, I was able to make it clear that I didn't think he was inadequate. He was then able to relax, stop hearing criticism, and learn new skills.

Shifting Perceptions

There's another magical benefit to skilled paraphrasing that encourages people to listen to you. You can actually shift the speaker's perception of what they said. When people misunderstand you or think you're out to get them, they can temporarily perceive you negatively and conveniently forget any past instances where you were helpful. They use words such as *always* or *never,* and see your past with them through a negative lens.

For instance, your employee doesn't like a training seminar she attended. She comes back and says, "You *always* waste my time by sending me to seminars that *never* have anything to do with my job. Since I've been hired, you just give me busywork and don't let me get ahead." But you notice that she's forgotten anything you've done that was helpful and simply sees you as "mean" throughout your shared history.

Once you're comfortable with using Basic and Advanced Ears, try employing the following two tools during conflicts to remind others that you wear a gray hat, not a black or white one.

Toolkit for Shifting Perceptions

1. Paraphrase a problem in the past tense. For example, your boss tells you that she doesn't believe that you're able to handle an important account. When you paraphrase, say something like, "So it sounds like *in the past* you *have felt* I couldn't handle this account well." By paraphrasing the problem in the past tense, you make it clear that the future may be different. You put the problems in the past and open up solutions for the future.

Read the example, and paraphrase the next two statements by putting them in the past tense:

Example Statement: You procrastinate and rush through a project even when you know the deadline is approaching.

Example Paraphrase: So it sounds like *in the past* you believe I've procrastinated and have *had* a problem with rushing through a project.

Statement: I've had feedback from other employees that you aren't a team player and you don't help others get their work done.
Your Paraphrase:

Statement: I don't want to work with Zelda because she doesn't follow through on her end of the project.
Your Paraphrase:

2. Paraphrase the problem and clarify that it's a partial truth rather than a whole truth. For example, when an employee tells you that you *never* give him a raise, you can say, "So your experience has been that I've *infrequently* given you raises." Paraphrasing a problem stressing the partial nature of a statement reminds the speaker that few situations in life are truly "always" or "never."

Read the following example, and paraphrase the problems from a whole truth to a partial truth:

Example Statement: You're *always* late to our meetings.
Example Paraphrase: It sounds like your experience is that I'm frequently late to our meetings.

Statement: You *never* get back to me with the information I request!
Your Paraphrase:

Statement: I *always* end up making the marketing phone calls because you *never* get around to it!
Your Paraphrase:

An Example of Shifting Perceptions

Brenda, a supervisor, was meeting with Joan, a difficult employee who was unhappy. "You never let me go to any workshops that advance my career," Joan complained. Brenda remembered the toolkit for shifting perceptions, and said, "So in the *past* you don't believe I've sent you to *enough* workshops that have been helpful to your career?" Joan paused and had to admit that she *had* been sent to one or two workshops that taught her some useful skills. As they continued to talk, the conversation now shifted from blaming Brenda to Joan confessing that she really wanted to attend a *specific* training seminar this year. Brenda ended up negotiating higher productivity and fewer complaints from Joan in exchange for attending the workshop.

Avoiding Arguments about Truth

A good listener points out underlying emotions and hidden agendas, then shifts perceptions in order to open up possibilities for negotiation. When you paraphrase people, you help them see that their own world is only truth with a small "t" and not the Truth for everyone. We're fond of believing that what we think should be universally true, but two individuals arguing about what's true only serves to generate unnecessary suffering. Instead, if people *owned* their thoughts, feelings, and experiences, there would be much less conflict, perhaps even less war. Owning our "Truth" means that we realize that it may be ours alone, and other people may see the same issue quite differently than we do.

I remember paraphrasing a friend one time, and every time I said, "So it sounds like you think . . ." he kept responding, "No! That's not what I think. That's the Truth!" However, as I kept paraphrasing and using the pronoun *you,* my friend admitted that what he was saying was true for *him.* It occurred to him as I paraphrased that maybe others might be seeing the situation in another way.

Other people may not agree that it's their opinion when you add the word *you.* However, it will remind you that Truth is never a good argument since "the truth" is always subjective. There's *my* truth and *your* truth and sometimes *our* truth. So you're wasting your breath if you're trying to prove Truth.

Of course, there are times when you might get a great deal of agreement on your truth if you take a public-opinion poll. But even in situations where you *could* win a poll on your point of view, arguments about Truth still don't work.

When I teach performance appraisals, I encourage managers

to forget about arguing Truth with employees. Nobody wins. Instead, state what you want as *your* truth. For instance, most of us in the West will agree that employees should be on time for work. Well, let's say you have a problem with a tardy employee. If you state *your* truth rather than arguing *the* Truth, you might say, "If you worked for another manager, punctuality might not be a big deal, but it's critical for *me*. If employees are on time when they work with me, I trust them; when they're late, I don't. I realize that this is something not every employer would expect. You have the right to work for another manager who doesn't care about punctuality. However, if you want to work for me, you'll have to figure out how to be on time."

You've now avoided the entire debate about whether or not what you're saying is *true* and whether what you want is *reasonable*. You've also made the employee responsible for shaping up or moving on.

Men, Passion, and Listening

Men often have trouble being *really* heard by women or *really* hearing women because most guys aren't taught to express their feelings. I find that my male clients have unique challenges in learning to use their new listening skills to connect to the women they love. The way men are taught not to have emotions in our culture was made obvious to me one hot summer day as I watched a barefoot three-year-old boy and his father walking along a hot sidewalk. The little boy was crying because his tender feet were sizzling. The father kept saying to his son, "Quit crying and stop acting like a girl!" Exasperated, the father finally stopped, looked directly at the little boy, and told his son in a firm voice, "Knock it off! There's *nothing* wrong!" Perhaps you can see why it can be very puzzling for women when we ask the men in our life what's wrong and they say, "Nothing!"

Most women deeply crave being emotionally *understood* and *understanding* the feelings of guys they find attractive. I remember when I first started dating my husband, Bruce, I exclaimed in frustration on a fourth date, "But I *really* want to know about your *inner* life." He answered me (only half-jokingly), "What *inner* life?" Many men don't realize that for women, a man's ability to express empathy (experiencing how someone else feels) and reveal his own emotions is the essential foundation for a passionate sexual connection.

I've often had male clients who are considered "nice guys" puzzle over why women fall head over heels for articulate guys who are "bad boys." I explain to them that many women find emotional expressiveness extremely seductive. Women want an emotional connection so badly that they often don't look *closely* at men who romance them with extraordinary listening. "Bad boys" don't follow most rules, including the cultural idea that "men don't express feelings," so *they* end up getting women's attention. But you don't have to be a bad boy to seduce your sweetheart.

If you're a guy who wants passion and attention from women, then use the Advanced Ears tool to help develop your ability to express your emotions. To make it easier to figure out what your woman is feeling, the next time she's talking, think about how *you'd* feel if you were going through what she's explaining. Now paraphrase the emotions she might feel by describing what *you'd* feel. Keep in mind that a paraphrase or amplification is a guess, so no one will sue you for being wrong. Also realize that sometimes you'll be right, and that it may be a touchy issue she's in denial about. If this occurs, your honey will at least realize on some level that you know the truth.

For example, your girlfriend might say, "So, darling, I was wondering if you want to spend next Christmas with my family," when what she's *really* wondering is whether you and she are a committed couple. If you just dive into a decision about Christmas, you'll miss what she's actually *trying* to say. If you use Advanced Ears, you might reply, "So it sounds like it's important to you that the two of us spend Christmas with your family? Can you tell me more?"

My husband jokes with me that men really do need a book of translation for "women speak" because we say "Go!" when we mean "Stay," along with so many other confusing messages. If you use Advanced Ears, you'll have that translation book that men keep looking for.

⁖ O ⁖

In this chapter you've learned a lot:

- How to get people to listen to you by managing touchy issues many of us deny

- How to clarify misunderstandings

- Ways to shift negative perceptions of yourself by others

- Tools for avoiding useless arguments about Truth

- Why listening is one of the sexiest activities a guy can engage in with his sweetheart

As you use your new tools to shift others' perceptions, you'll find that many people won't believe that you're qualified to change their point of view unless you can first demonstrate that you understand how they see the world. As you listen intently, you'll be surprised to discover profound differences in how each of us perceives the same issues. You may start to suspect that it's not just that men and women come from different planets, but that we all live in separate universes. You may then begin wondering how to bridge these vast chasms of perceptions.

In the next chapter, you'll find out how these unique personal worlds develop as everyone grows up in different tribes (families). You'll learn how to see these tribal differences, and communicate so that it won't matter what universe someone else comes from— you'll still know a language that will work . . . universally.

CHAPTER 8

INFLUENCING
PEOPLE

*"The greatest problem in communication is
the illusion that it has been accomplished."*
— Daniel W. Davenport

Social Sorcery isn't a natural talent. Our "normal" communication habits are formed in the family we grew up in. We may refine ways of relating to others throughout our life, but families hardwire us for certain automatic ways of engaging others.

These days everybody seems to have come from a family that was "dysfunctional" in some way. One of my friends, Sara, who has a wry sense of humor, likes to say that her eccentric family put the "fun" in "dysfunctional." Even though most families have problems, people still feel a strong loyalty to their kin.

When you first consider that your family might not have been ideal, it can be quite disturbing. Whenever I'd write anything that implied that parents can teach kids poor communication habits, one of my editors used to joke, "Now, Skube, don't go saying noth-in' bad about my mama!" But he was only partly kidding because it can be upsetting to consider that people you love so much can make mistakes.

For the record, families teach us both effective *and* ineffective ways to connect, but having the Interpersonal Edge is about keeping what's useful and having a choice about changing what's not.

Breaking the Family Spell

You may have learned that when people do something nice for you, it's a good idea to thank them. This behavior is certainly functional. On the other hand, you may have learned that if you want something, the best way to get it is to pout. I come from a long line of champion pouters. Of course, as an adult I found that people didn't respond well to my "normal" pouting communica-tion. At first I tried to pout with more intensity or frequency. I figured if a technique didn't work, I'd do it more or harder.

At one point, it became obvious that I needed to discontinue my loyalty to my family's "art of pouting." However, when I tried to say what I wanted, it felt unnatural, and I wasn't good at it. I also figured, erroneously, that if anyone really cared, they should *know* what I wanted because it would save me having to ask and then feeling embarrassed if someone said no. As time went on, I noticed something significant about *asking* rather than pout-ing—I might not be looking cool or feeling groovy, but I was actu-ally getting what I wanted more often.

Being grateful to your family for the useful rituals they taught you is a good idea, since gratitude in any form is powerful. Being grateful forces us to focus on what's positive in our life and can also make this good thing expand. Since you don't need help with what your family did *right,* this chapter focuses on the rituals your family taught you that *don't* work. But focusing on the bad stuff won't make it expand; it will simply give you the option to stop doing what isn't working.

Understanding Your Tribe

Imagine that we're all from different tribes. We call these tribes "families," but they might as well be foreign cultures. Anyone who's been married knows the difficulty involved in blending their spouse's family customs with their own, such as: how conflict is handled, how boys are treated versus girls, or how birthdays are celebrated. Every time you interact with another person, you're facing a possible clash of cultures. This relationship culture shock is based on three beliefs:

1. We tend to assume that other people have the same customs that we do.

2. We don't question the value of our own customs.

3. When we do see differences, we believe that others' customs are silly.

I remember a friend of mine, Joe, who married a woman, Gail, who always carved off the sides of the turkey before baking it on Thanksgiving. One holiday he decided to ask his wife about this custom. She replied that she'd learned it from her mother. He then went into the living room to ask the mother the same question, who replied that she didn't know and referred him to the grandmother. He looked at the grandmother and asked the same question. The grandmother replied, "When I was a young girl, we had a small oven, and a large turkey wouldn't fit without having the sides cut off." My friend was amused to learn that the custom had been passed down to each generation without considering the size of the current oven available for the turkey. When we don't question family customs, we end up feeling like this turkey—carved down and limited to fit an obsolete need.

Family customs create problems for us as adults when they become automatic and unconscious. We're hurt when other people don't do the "right" thing on our birthday. We're mad that our spouse doesn't have the "right" ritual for resolving a fight. We withdraw when a friend violates the "right" way to be our buddy. We also confuse other people because we're busy being good members of our own tribe and following rules that other people don't even know about.

For instance, my client Jerry learned as a kid that he was always supposed to look happy no matter what he was really feeling. Now, as an adult, he has trouble telling people what he wants or is feeling, and he's always vaguely unhappy but doesn't know why. People who know Jerry sense his unhappiness and feel confused because he almost always puts on a happy face. After therapy with me, he finally realized that he had the option to stop pretending he was constantly happy.

Another client, Ariel, used to complain bitterly about the "thoughtlessness" of other people. She was overly helpful, generous, and nice because in her family everyone bent over backward for each other. But in the real world, she ended up being a doormat. People were perfectly willing to take from her, but didn't share her tribal custom of being obligated to give back. When Ariel was able to see that other people didn't share her rules, she began to only give to people who she knew would not take advantage of her generosity. So, she stopped feeling furious and started to feel appreciated.

Inner Peace

To get along with others, we also need to realize that we're not just navigating external tribal differences. As each of us grew up, we developed an "inner tribe" of colorful personalities that often disagreed.

For instance, as a kid you may have watched your mom bake mouth-watering cookies that she told you not to eat until after dinner. The part of you that wanted to be a "good kid" would tell you not to eat any of the cookies. The part of you that really wanted to bite into the luscious sweetness would argue that "just one" wouldn't hurt. In cartoons, these separate selves are often represented by a devil on one of our shoulders and an angel on the other, debating what we should do.

The selves or personalities we all possess develop out of, and are a mirror of, the rules of the tribe we grew up in. The inner voices that tell us how we *should* and *shouldn't* act are like whispers from these internal personas. Sometimes our inside selves obey our family traditions, but we don't always develop an inner tribe that agrees with our outer clan. We also have "rebel selves" that fight against our family rules. The therapist's child who acts "crazy" or the minister's child who "runs wild" are examples of a rebel self taking charge.

It's important that you're aware of your inner tribe, because good relationships in your outside world start with good relationships among your inner selves. No soul ends up with any inner peace if these selves are not understood, because they control your behavior outside of your awareness. When we argue with ourselves about what jobs to take and whether to go back to school, have a baby, or leave a marriage—the voice of every personality within our inner tribe needs to be heard.

In some early Native American tribes, the tribal elders would only make a decision when complete agreement among the group was achieved. The elders knew that resolving conflicts among the individual personalities would result in the best decision. Similarly, in your own inner tribe, if you can't hear *all* your selves, you'll have ongoing inner battles and chronic trouble with effective decision making.

My client Darwin felt as if he were "trapped" in a passionless marriage. As he engaged in therapy with me, he met parts of himself that were frightened and that valued safety above all else. His parents had taught him that he should avoid taking risks, never consider divorce, and always try to please others. But he was miserable because he also had inner selves that wanted him to relax and be himself with his wife. If he risked telling his wife what he *really* wanted, he feared that she might not love him anymore. Then again, he just might get the passion and intimacy he'd been longing for. As he got to know his inner tribe, his "frightened self" and "passionate self" were able to negotiate their separate agendas. Darwin was then able to take the risks with his wife that, to his surprise, resulted in the emotional and erotic relationship he'd craved.

Our separate selves can create battles where we get stuck between our head and our heart. We all know actions that we *should* take that would improve our lives, such as losing weight, being more patient with our kids, or exercising. However, getting our heart to agree with our head requires seeing the difference between our intellectual self and our emotional self. Many clients come into my coaching or therapy practice trying to intellectually force the process. They grunt, groan, and apply major discipline—and get nowhere. The heart is a different planet, with different laws from the intellect. When our intellectual selves are informed by our emotional selves, we make wise choices. But we can't manage our emotional selves by treating them as part of our thinking process.

To resolve the internal conflicts you have with yourself and the external conflicts you have with others, a good understanding of your family customs is essential. Following is a list of typical family rituals or behaviors, and samples of the inner selves that can develop when we have these experiences:

Family Rituals	Explanation
Lots of criticism	"I'm never good enough."
"Nothing's wrong."	"I can't believe what I experience."
Little affection or touching	"I'm not lovable."
"Wipe that look off your face!"	"Something is wrong with my feelings."
"Children should be seen and not heard."	"I shouldn't express myself."
"Stop crying or I'll give you something to cry about."	"It's dangerous to show I'm sad."
"Shame on you!"	"Something's wrong with me."
"I did it for your own good."	"People hurt me when they love me."

As you can see, most of us develop some pretty wacky beliefs through which we interpret the actions and words of other people. Unfortunately, we don't even know that we're distorting information. Instead, we think that people are really telling us that we aren't good enough, aren't lovable, or are bad.

I often listen to clients making absolute statements about other people's behavior. My client Anna was recently telling me that her nephew "scolded" her. I kept asking how she knew his intent, and she became furious that I was "questioning her credibility." She finally saw that my questions weren't about her reliability, but about her automatic assumptions. Anna realized that she didn't know her nephew's intent since she was too furious about her assumptions to ask him.

As children, we get used to the repeated messages and behaviors of our parents. As adults, we either distort current relationships so that we perceive others as doing what our family did, or we re-create our family relationships with everyone (or both). For example, if we grew up in an angry family and believe everyone is always mad at us, we may constantly ask people what *they're* mad about. After a while, people will blow up at us—not because they were originally mad, but because our repeated questioning has pissed them off. Voilà, we're back in our family! Moreover, everyone else has similar habitual distortions and is misinterpreting us.

New therapy clients sometimes come in and tell me they had a perfect childhood and don't understand why they feel so miserable. One client, Gary, said to me in the beginning of therapy, "My family couldn't have had any problems; we all dressed so well." It took a couple of years before he saw that the custom of perfection in his narcissistic family was the problem.

In executive coaching, clients are often amazed once they see how family rituals have influenced their behavior at work. Ben, one supervisor I worked with, was the oldest child of three siblings whose parents were usually gone and placed him in charge. When his mom and dad would return home, his younger siblings complained about Ben, and his parents would get upset.

As an adult, Ben was frequently the acting manager for his department. Predictably, when the boss returned, his co-workers would complain about Ben, and his boss would chew him out. Ben was repeating his childhood because he was still acting like a child who couldn't confront his parents. Due to my advice, he finally met with his boss and said, "If you want me to be in charge while you're gone, then I need you to trust my decisions. If you don't want to give me this authority, then please make one of my co-workers acting manager."

His boss quickly agreed to start supporting Ben and keep him as acting manager, since none of his co-workers were as competent. He was only able to resolve his dilemma when he could break the spell of his childhood customs with his parents.

Toolkit for Inner Peace

Complete the following exercise in order to identify customs you learned in your family that influence your current relationships:

1. Write down the names of one or two people in your life today who really annoy you.

2. Describe how you feel or think when you're around these people:

3. Was there anyone in your family that you felt this way around? Who?

Compare the people who bother you today and those who did so in your past. What family customs, beliefs, or inner selves might be contributing to your distress? For example, did you feel overlooked as a kid, have an inner self that believed you were boring, or do you get upset with people today who appear thoughtless? If you can see that many negative messages about yourself were merely ideas you adopted in your childhood, then you can see that these beliefs were merely the *opinions* of the people who raised you. You, then, won't have to continue to act as if these thoughts were true or be as bothered by those who upset you in the same way that your family members did.

An Example of Inner Peace

Candace couldn't stand her mother-in-law, Betty, or her neighbor, Julia. She always felt small, inept, and untrustworthy when she talked to either of these women. Using this toolkit, she realized that she felt the same way around her dad. He was stern, loud, and disapproving throughout most of her childhood, and she'd always been scared of him. From then on, when she had to deal with Betty and Julia, she first reminded herself that these people were not her dad, and she wasn't small anymore. Betty and Julia still weren't her favorite people, but she could now interact with them calmly and with dignity.

The Price of Being Comfortably Numb

Frequently, the result of family traditions is that people decide that certain emotions are off-limits. For example, think about the four emotional categories: *glad, sad, mad,* and *scared.* In your family, how was each emotion expressed? Were certain feelings discouraged or suppressed? Maybe happiness and sadness were okay, but anger was verboten. A great deal of unnecessary suffering results when we numb out feelings that we *think* we shouldn't have. You can't have an effective emotional relationship with others when you don't have an effective emotional relationship with yourself.

In general, many families in our culture discourage some emotions and don't give their kids solid "emotional educations" about how to deal with intense feelings. Our collective lack of training in this area creates pervasive social problems as well as individual misery. Some researchers believe that the current epidemic of addictive behaviors is related to our inability or refusal to feel our emotions. Many 12-step programs talk about people trying to fill the hole in their soul with an addiction.

The specialty areas in my business are interpersonal relationships at work and home, intrapersonal relationships (our relationship with our *insides*), and addictions, because people who can't connect within themselves typically can't connect to others. If we can't establish relationships with ourselves first, then others, we tend to form addictive relationships with either substances (drugs and alcohol) or compulsive behaviors (binge eating and becoming a workaholic). People become dangerous, and addiction becomes safe because we'd rather *depend* on a substance or compulsive behavior than *need* other people and get rejected.

Many 12-step programs and therapy for addictions work because the former addict learns how to stop depending on substances or compulsive behaviors and start depending on people instead. When our emotional needs are met by others, our need to "numb out" or "fill up" via an addiction is less appealing. If we're isolated and lack a community in which to express ourselves, we can literally kill ourselves trying to be comfortably numb. Accidental drug overdoses, diabetes caused by obsessive overeating, and sexual diseases contracted during compulsive affairs can put our lives on the line. To the extent that we remain isolated and without a community, we'll seek out addictions and compulsions. The advice "Just say no!" doesn't work if there's no one around to hear us say no.

Negotiating Tribal Differences

The normal reaction when a person notices tribal differences is to describe others with a three-letter word: B-A-D. Usually when we respond in this way, the other person feels ashamed, and withdraws or attacks.

I was at a retreat center recently and was putting together a piece of peanut-butter-and-jam toast for breakfast. As I was absent-mindedly applying my family's recipe: light butter, light peanut butter, and heavy jam—a woman at the retreat popped up behind me. Her mouth dropped open, and she exclaimed loudly, "You're putting *butter* on your *toast* with *peanut butter!*" Now I hadn't previously thought of this action as revolutionary. I nodded, and she repeated, "You're putting *butter* on your *toast* with *peanut butter!*" For several minutes she polled people drifting past us about their toast habits, and continued to express shock. I finally looked at her and said, "You know, I had previously planned to shock you by doing something like streaking around naked on the property, but I can see that streaking will be unnecessary. Instead, I shall simply put butter on my toast each morning." We both chuckled, and she returned to her table.

Like this woman, we're often amazed, dismayed, and disturbed when we see someone with a custom different from our own—we feel that our habits are being called into question. We may even feel the need to poll others, to be right, and to change the behavior of the other party.

I read an anonymous quote on the Internet the other day that said, "Anyone who drives slower than you is an idiot, and anyone who drives faster is a maniac." Of course, when we see people who are different as being wrong, nothing magical is going to happen, so let's look at tools that will help you negotiate tribal differences.

Toolkit for Negotiating Tribal Differences

Think of someone who communicates in a way that you find frustrating. Now imagine a family where this habit may have been useful. Ask yourself how this way of communicating may have helped this person as a child. Write down three benefits the person may have received from using this behavior.

An Example of Negotiating Tribal Differences

You can use the trick you just practiced every time someone's driving you crazy. The idea is to invent hypotheses that don't make the person "B-A-D." Let's say that your boss is a control freak. You probably think he stays up nights trying to make you feel inadequate, but what if he had a violent father and needed to make sure nothing went wrong around his dad? What if your boss's mom was drinking a lot and he needed to take care of her all the time, as well as raise his younger siblings? Can you see why your boss would feel constantly anxious trying to make sure nothing goes wrong?

If you can see these kinds of possibilities, the next time your boss acts controlling you might say, "I imagine it's important to you that nothing goes wrong. I can't promise you that nothing will go wrong, but I will promise you that I'll take the following steps and be very careful with the project."

In another situation, you might be a salesperson working for a small business where the CEO has her entire fortune riding on sales. When your boss calls you with daily criticisms, you might think she's a harpy. You could also be aware she might lose her house. You could then say, "Hey, I know you have everything riding on our sales, and the most I can lose is a job. I can't promise you that I can make the exact sales quota you need, but I'm doing everything I can to sell this product."

These reassuring statements don't take away anyone's upsetting history, but they do establish you as an ally, not an adversary. When we acknowledge another person's emotions, the individual often calms down and lowers the volume on their annoying behavior. Often the person we're addressing isn't even aware of their feeling until we state it. If we don't acknowledge the emotion, we can bend over backward to address the rational problem and the person will still drive us crazy.

Assuming the best about people's behavior will also calm *you* down, because you won't presume that others are out to get you or are personally attacking you.

∴ O ∴

Since imperfect human beings raise us, we all come through childhood with vulnerabilities. For instance, in your tribe every time your father disapproved of you, he may have raised an eyebrow and become quiet. In your adult life, if anyone raises an eyebrow and becomes quiet, you may assume they disapprove of you without your even asking them. Certain words, behaviors, and even tones of voice can be buried like land mines, waiting for unsuspecting feet to set off an explosion. If you consider the complexity of all these triggers interacting, it's amazing that anyone ever communicates effectively. The good news, once you see this dynamic, is that you can stop taking the behavior of other people personally. Two steps will assist you in not blowing up in your work and home connections:

1. *Ask* about others' motives rather than assuming you know.
Example: "Frank, when you raised your eyebrow in the meeting this morning and became quiet, I assumed you didn't like my proposal. Is that what you were thinking, or was something else going on?"

2. When you see people reacting strongly to you, ask questions to find out what they might be assuming about *your* behavior.
Example: "Sara, when I asked you about the meeting yesterday, you almost gagged on your doughnut. What were you thinking?"

Since you now know how to avoid the emotional land mines buried in conversations, you'll be able to use the next chapter to create specific formulas that will work wizardry in your unique circumstances, in order to get what you want.

CHAPTER 9

WORD WIZARDRY

"Words are, of course, the most powerful drug used by mankind."
— Rudyard Kipling

Tele-visioning

Tele-visioning is when you precisely state the behaviors you want or don't want to see in another person. Imagine that you were writing stage direction for an actor. The language wouldn't state: "Actress leaves." It would be precise, as in "The actress exits stage left." When you Tele-vision, you tell others what you'd see if their behavior were on TV.

Words can be interpreted in numerous ways by different people. We believe that they know what we mean when we use words such as *trust, integrity,* or *respect.* For instance, you may believe that trust means that you don't ask questions because that's what it meant when you were growing up. In another family, however, you might have to ask questions to demonstrate trust.

One of my clients calls these abstract terms "marshmallow" words, because the definitions are so soft and mushy. For instance, someone might be angry with you and say you're "impossible." Unless you get details about what specific behavior is offending this person, you'll flounder around with all sorts of wrong ideas.

When I work in organizations, I often notice employees trying to fix people problems without knowing what behavior is causing the conflict. Felicia, a tall client of mine, did this before she worked with me. She was told by her manager that she was intimidating, so she decided that her problem had to be that she was too tall. As a result, she proceeded to slump. By the time she started coaching sessions with me, she had a back problem, and her manager still had the same complaint.

After seeing me a few times, Felicia realized that her tendency to challenge her boss by questioning him aggressively during meetings was the actual issue. She learned to engage in private conversations with him, and received a glowing review at her next evaluation. Her back pain and discomfort at work cleared up.

The film *Love Story* provides a great example of marshmallow words in romantic affairs. On her deathbed, Ali MacGraw's character, Jenny, intones the now-famous line to Ryan O'Neal's character, Oliver: "Love means never having to say you're sorry." It was a touching scene, but let's be honest, "never having to say you're sorry" is a pretty limited description of love. Moreover, our current divorce rate of approximately 50 percent shows that staying married must require more willingness to apologize than most couples realize.

Men and women typically get themselves into a lot of trouble by using marshmallow words. While doing couples therapy, I often see one spouse insisting that the other doesn't know how to express love. In one case, I asked my client Denise, "What exactly would your husband do if he really loved you? Without hesitating, Denise replied, "He'd go hiking with me." Now that wouldn't have been everyone's definition of love, but it helped this couple end a serious fight.

Read the following scenario and notice how confusing the marshmallow words make communication. The poorly defined terms are italicized.

Jill: "I don't think you *respect* my work."

Bill: "Of course I *respect* your work. You do a *great* job."

Jill: "No, you don't *understand* what I'm saying. You never listen to me or take me *seriously*."

At the end of this discussion, it's unlikely that Bill or Jill have any idea what behaviors they're talking about. They can't resolve the argument without knowing the specific actions that are creating the problem. Let's run the scenario again using the Social Sorcery tool of Tele-visioning:

Jill: "Bill, I find it difficult to express my ideas if I'm *interrupted* in a meeting."

Bill: "I didn't know it bothered you. I was trying to *give you more information*."

Jill: "I'd find it more helpful if you would *wait until after I finished my idea* and then make your point."

With the Tele-visioning technique, you describe concrete behaviors without attaching your interpretations about *why* the person is doing something. Most people find it hard to stop attributing motives to other people's actions. Many of us can remember in elementary school when someone who was disliked was called silly names. Then people grow up and discover more refined insults like "arrogant" or "oppositional." I find that many clients use these sophisticated words and *believe* they're effectively "communicating" their thoughts. In reality, other people will just feel as insulted as if you'd called them a "pig" on the playground, and they still don't know what you want. For example, if you tell your friend that he's "unsupportive," he's only heard that you think he's "bad." He still doesn't know that you want him to listen to you talk about the rotten day you had.

Social Sorcerers work hard to avoid making up stuff about people's behavior. If someone turns her back to you, you can decide that she's being a "snob." Then again, she might simply want to look in the other direction. The more you speak about behavior and the less you randomly interpret what it means, the closer you get to a form of magical communication.

Imagine that your co-worker keeps excluding you from a critical meeting at the end of each week. You can talk to her about "undermining" you, or you can discuss why she didn't send you an e-mail regarding the meeting. The language that refers to the missing e-mail will tell your co-worker what you want, *and* she won't feel insulted.

The Tele-visioning technique works like this: Imagine that the person is doing what you want or don't want on a television screen. What physical behaviors do you see? Now, describe them to the other person. If you've never tried this before, it may be difficult at first. When I recently asked my client Martha to Tele-vision, she said, "I want to be understood." I shook my head and asked for specifics, so she added, "I want a sense that I'm being listened to and respected." That was close, but when I finally got Martha to Tele-vision, she said, "I'd like eye contact when I'm speaking, no interruptions, and understanding noises [such as *uh-huh*] and head nods." Now Martha was finally Tele-visioning. Because she was now able to articulate the specific behaviors she was looking for, her odds of getting what she wanted increased tenfold.

When we choose words such as *selfish, stubborn,* or *unreasonable,* we guarantee that people will feel judged by us. Even when we use lofty psychological terms like "passive-aggressive," people still feel criticized. Rather than "You're being *selfish,*" you could say, "I'd like it if you'd leave some ice cream for me." Rather than "You're being *stubborn,*" you could say, "I want to see the movie of my choice this weekend." Rather than "Stop being *unreasonable,*" you could try, "I want you to listen to my point of view." The key to Tele-visioning is that you focus on *requesting* behavior, not on blaming the listener.

Toolkit for Tele-visioning

Write down three things people do that you find irritating, and use marshmallow words to describe what you don't like: (example: *ranting, being a jerk,* or *ignoring me*).

Now close your eyes, see the specific *behaviors* of this person on a television screen, and rewrite them in Tele-visioning language: (example: *using a loud voice, taking the last cookie,* or *not returning calls*).

Look for daily opportunities to practice the Tele-visioning technique with friends, family members, and co-workers until you feel comfortable with it.

An Example of Tele-visioning

Serena was sick of the nightly fights at the dinner table whenever she tried to teach her three kids proper table manners. She usually nagged them by saying, "Quit eating like animals and use good manners!" One evening she tried the Tele-visioning tool: "Elbows off the table, plate under your chin, one person talks at a time, use your utensils, and wipe your face with your napkin—or forget about dessert!" After her kids got over the shock of *finally* being given specific instructions, they complied. No more dinner wars!

Tele-visioning works best when it's a "two-way street." Use it when you talk to others, and ask others to use it when they talk to you. "Give me an example," is a million-dollar question when others are being vague. No matter how many times someone calls you "a jerk," asking for examples will eventually force a behavioral description of what the person wants.

A corporate group I've worked with for a long time loves the concept of "marshmallow" words. All of the participants are practiced Social Sorcerers. When we get together, they're fond of bringing bags of marshmallows and tossing them at whoever is being vague during the meeting. It lightens up the mood and increases awareness at the same time. Occasionally, there are times when we use vague words in the meeting and nobody tosses marshmallows. It's not necessary to have surgical preciseness in language 100 percent of the time. Marshmallow language works fine when all you're saying is, "What a great day." However, during conflicts or negotiations, precise language is critically important.

The Enchantment of Saying "I"

Wouldn't it be great to have magical authority over others and know that another person couldn't challenge your point of view? Moreover, imagine that this enchanting communication defuses defensiveness, encourages listening, and creates rapport. Does this sound like sorcery? Well, keep reading! "I" language is a tool that encourages you to talk about your own perceptions, your own experience, and your own feelings. How it works is that you start out most sentences with "I" and avoid starting sentences with "You." When using "I" language, it's fine to have the pronoun "you" in your communication—just don't start with it.

Here are two examples that will show you why "I" language is enchanting. In the first, the marshmallow words are in italics to highlight that "you" language makes it more likely you'll use vague and blaming language. The Tele-visioning words are bolded in the "I" language example. Notice that the "I" language example does use some vague words such as *frustrated,* and *help,* however, these particular terms aren't used to describe the problem or the solution.

- "You" language: "You aren't a *team player* and you don't *respect* the needs of other people in your office. You're obviously not interested in being seen as a *contributor* here at Worldwide Business, Inc."

- "I" language: "I've noticed you've **missed several team meetings** and **your reports** to your co-workers are usually **late.** I'm frustrated because we need your help. I'd like to talk about what you need to **be at the meetings,** or whether you want to be **reassigned to a different project.**

Tele-visioning and "I" language go hand in hand. These two tools avoid blaming, encourage participation, and are specific about problem behaviors. In addition, when you use "I," you speak with ultimate authority. Other people can say you *shouldn't* feel, think, or perceive what you're telling them, but *you* have an airtight defense. You can paraphrase them, repeating back, "So you don't think that I *should* feel this way?" You then can use Tele-visioning and "I" language to describe the experience you're having regardless of *their* truth. When you use the word "I," you stay out of arguments about the *Truth* and share *your* truth.

I realize that everyone probably likes their truth a lot, and may even think every reasonable person agrees with them, but no matter how devoted you are to your truth, you'll create enemies, not converts, if you force your beliefs down others' throats. The minute you talk about the other person rather than yourself, you lose ultimate authority. You are, however, the ultimate expert on yourself.

"I" language is more than just a trick of word usage. Using "I" at the beginning of a sentence means that you're taking responsibility for your own thoughts, feelings, and experiences. When you do so, you immediately increase the probability of being heard. Other people hear you talking about yourself without any pressure to agree with your viewpoint.

Using "I" language does require more self-knowledge and self-disclosure. Saying "I want you to listen to my point of view" requires you to know what you need and take the risk of being turned down. Saying "You're thoughtless and pigheaded" doesn't require much self-knowledge, but it does risk permanently alienating the listener (or being smacked if the listener is impulsive).

There's one exception to using the formula of putting "I" at the beginning of your sentences that also works wonders in conversations. The formula is direct, easy for people to understand, and nonblaming:

"When you did _____, I felt _____, and what I'd like instead is_____."

For example, "When you tell me I'm being *irrational,* I feel *irritated,* and what I'd like instead is *for you to tell me what it is you really wanted!"*

Many times we don't let people know what we want and expect them to guess at what *would* work. By readily giving them the answer, you help people give you what you want. My young daughter has a little girlfriend who likes to use an abandonment tactic to get what she wants. When the girls are playing together, I'll watch this little girl turn her back and say, "I don't want to be your friend anymore," then huff away. I'll intervene, get the girls together, and tell my daughter to ask her friend what she wants. Usually she just wants my daughter to play her favorite game. My daughter now knows to tell her little friend, "I'm going to play with someone else for a while if you turn away and won't tell me what you want." Then my daughter will play by herself or with another buddy. Her friend has gotten quite good at saying what she wants, and drops her abandonment routine when she's around my daughter. However, she still uses abandonment on other kids who don't ask her to communicate what she wants.

A word of warning: People can use "I" language to hide an insult or to blame. Example: "*I* have noticed you're a jerk." Using "I" language in this way isn't magical—you'll only succeed at making people mad. Therefore, don't use the word "I" to point out someone's character flaws. Instead, describe specific behavior. Saying, "*I* think you're rude" is easier but less effective than figuring out the *behavior* you don't like. Saying "I get distracted when you keep looking at your watch and glancing over your shoulder; can we set up a different time to talk?" will focus on what you *want,* not on what's wrong with the other person.

Toolkit for the Enchantment of Saying "I"

Take the following sentences and turn "You" language into "I" language. Remember that "I" language focuses on requesting *behavior* you'd like.

Example:

- **"You"**: "You constantly snub me and plan stuff behind my back!"

- **"I"**: "I'd like to be invited to your next department meeting."

- **"You"**: "You're really controlling, and I'm sick of being bossed around."

- **"I"**: I [your example]

- **"You"**: "You're so selfish and think the world revolves around you!"

- **"I"**: I [your example]

- **"You"**: "You're so obsessive! Could you just chill out?"

- **"I"**: I [your example]

Exploring Inner Space

When you want to influence people, you'll find that your most powerful tool is self-knowledge. If you're blind to what you're doing, you won't understand the results you're getting. When we hide big parts of ourselves from others, it's usually because we feel embarrassed. We may think that other people would negatively judge us if they knew us better. When you have the Interpersonal Edge, you'll see relationships as opportunities to reveal mysterious aspects of yourself and others. As you practice the tools in this book, you'll find that "inner space" is a powerful and underexplored frontier.

A good model for understanding the "inner spaces" in relationships is called the Johari Window. There are four quadrants in this model: open, blind, hidden, and unknown. The open quadrant is what you know and others know (that is, you have brown hair). The blind quadrant is what others know and you're oblivious to (for example, you have a "kick me" sign on your back). The hidden quadrant is sensitive information that you know but you don't tell others (that is, you secretly surf porn on the Internet). The unknown quadrant is stuff neither you nor others know about you (for instance, your great-great-great-grandfather was manic-depressive). We assume the unknown area exists because eventually some of these things become known, and we then realize that these behaviors and motives were influencing relationships all along.

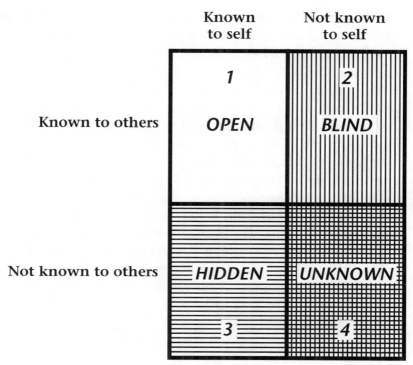

Johari Window

When you seek to influence others, you'll need to use tools that help you expand your open area (where you and others know the same information), and shrink the blind, hidden, and unknown areas. Alcoholics Anonymous says that people are only as sick as their secrets. When you tell your secrets to appropriate, trustworthy people, you reduce your isolation and shame. Psychologist and author Harriet Lerner was once asked if her practice of passing her childhood diaries around in some classes she teaches was embarrassing. She said, "When you reach fifty, your life is no longer embarrassing, because you realize that everyone's life is embarrassing." There's something about sharing our hidden areas with others that allows us to build connections through our imperfections. You'll also find that paraphrasing can help people hear your feedback about their blind areas with less defensiveness, since the words you're repeating came from them.

Imagine that you're blindfolded and are standing next to an elephant, but you don't know what you're touching. You're holding on to the tail and you say you're feeling a leathery sort of rope. Your blindfolded spouse is standing next to a leg and describes a "leathery tree." A blindfolded friend is standing next to the elephant's trunk and describes "a giant hose." Together, the three of you would eventually figure out that the creature is an elephant—but you could only do so by sharing data. When it comes to the hard work of exploring inner space, we need all the help we can get. When you increase your openness to appropriate others, you increase the amount of help you can receive to create a greater understanding of yourself, your soul, and your world.

If you use "I" language and Tele-visioning, you'll greatly improve the odds that most people will *want* to listen to you. You'll also notice that there are certain difficult people with whom every communication tool you try will backfire. The next chapter will show you how to spot, deal with, or exit relationships with those who are "impossible."

CHAPTER 10

IMPOSSIBLE PEOPLE

"Time wounds all heels."
— Jane Sherwood Ace

In my experience, there are two primary forces that affect human relationships: love and fear. I think of love as being an actual physical force that promotes aliveness, attachment, and consciousness. I think of fear as being an opposite physical force that promotes numbness, apathy, and unconsciousness. Every day in every decision we make, we choose between these two influences. If the majority of our choices supports aliveness, we align ourselves with love. If the majority supports unconsciousness, we align ourselves with fear.

Dangerous Liaisons

I find that many of my clients get into trouble when they operate *as if* everyone only has good intentions. They then end up like Charlie Brown, repeatedly trying to kick a football that Lucy is holding . . . then pulling away at the last second. Sometimes other people set us up to fail. If we see their plan, we can stop trying to kick the ball.

Vampires and demons who inspire fear may merely inhabit the realm of myth. Then again, some folks we encounter can seem so devoted to terrorizing us that we start to believe in these myths! And if combating scary people *externally* wasn't enough, on a bad day we may think that an exorcist could be useful to rid us of our own self-criticism.

This chapter will show you how to deal with both destructive people "out there" and our self-critical "inner predator," which is a part of us that can hate, criticize, and sabotage ourselves better than anyone else can. If *you* can't recognize the inner voices that are abusing you, it's even more difficult to effectively protect yourself from the people in your life who are doing so. Fighting an external foe skillfully is only possible when you aren't simultaneously undermining yourself from within.

Many spiritual traditions consider the earth to be a place where free will reigns. Free will means that you get to choose the light side of the Force (love) or hang out with Darth Vader (fear). Everybody has the same choice. Recognizing whom you're dealing with is critical to having the Interpersonal Edge.

Now, just because your annoying brother likes to bug you, it doesn't mean he's in cahoots with the Dark Lord. Many of us demonize others when we feel uncomfortable around them. Most of the people you've demonized will lose their tail and horns when you use Social Sorcery. However, some folks will look even more dangerous than you first imagined. Being able to tell who has malicious intentions might make you nervous, but it can also save you much unnecessary suffering.

The toolkits you've learned will optimize your chances of creating supportive relationships *and* make it obvious when you're dealing with people who chose fear over love. Sometimes my clients think that being a spiritual person means they should be able to transform Vampires into angels. I point out to them that nobody gets to mess with free will. However, we *do* get to choose whom we want to hang out with.

I've noticed that our culture has many odd beliefs that encourage sacrifice and martyrdom. I tell my clients that the main thing to pay attention to in the word *martyrdom* is the dumb part. Sacrificing yourself to feed Vampires strengthens the predators. Sacrificing yourself to your inner predator will strengthen the self-destructive part of you.

Social Sorcerers work at relationships from both the inner and outer levels. Addressing your inner world and then addressing your outer relationships will give you more power, influence, and options. If you deny or don't see the self-destructive part of you, then you'll likely deny the part of others that is destructive.

People who venerate fear can be hard to spot since they don't necessarily wear black, look gothic, and sport fangs. You'll recognize them more easily by their *constant* pursuit of power and desire to control everyone. With the Interpersonal Edge, you'll know that real power comes from control of yourself, not others. It's especially critical that you stay in charge of yourself around people who operate like Vampires. Otherwise, they can suck the aliveness out of you, create chaos, and feed on your fear or anger. You don't want to encourage connection with Vampires because they'll use the closeness to access your neck.

However, close relationships in your life will dispel Vampires like garlic, as they seek out people who are isolated, lonely, and ashamed of their needs. Western culture has made it easier for Vampires to maneuver by revering autonomy, independence, and self-sufficiency. Regardless of what the old song exclaims, we don't always see people who need other people as "the luckiest people in the world." Rather, we tend to see them as weak, unsuccessful wimps. Destructive people will look for your weaknesses—and exploit them. If you're ashamed of your needs, you leave the door wide open to being preyed upon. If you know and have accepted your vulnerabilities, you don't leave external or internal demons much room to operate.

Having the Interpersonal Edge means that you're able to accept your normal need to interact with others. This can be tricky, since "dependency" in Western culture is viewed with suspicion. In my doctoral dissertation, I made the point that most of the standard mental-health tests don't even include measures of social skills, ability to cooperate, or to be interdependent. Through my research, I found that the people who scored the highest on the standard measurements of mental health were extremely *independent*. However, when I put them together in a work group, they couldn't even cooperate long enough to finish a simple project.

Research shows that Western parents promote independence as a primary goal for their children. Moms and dads brag about how fast their kids walked, talked, or were potty trained. Most of us want children to mature quickly because we think that kids shouldn't be dependent on their thumbs, diapers, or even their hands when they're learning to walk on "their own two feet." One of the highest compliments for many parents is to hear how independent their children are. One of the worst insults is to tell parents that their kids appear to be needy. In short, mainstream culture trains people to be Lone Rangers. Then we wonder why we don't know how to connect with others and end up being vulnerable to abusers of one sort or another.

What If Somebody Threw a Power Struggle and Nobody Came?

It would be nice if you could walk out into the world and ask the Vampires to raise their hands so that you could avoid them. Fortunately, there *are* two traits that make Vampires easier to spot:

1. They want power not love, so they live for power struggles.

2. Mirrors give Vampires away because the undead have no ability to reflect. The undead in real life are unable to reflect on their own behavior or meet the needs of people around them—even if they receive direct, specific requests.

Since being in control feeds Vampires, if you learn how to make direct requests and stop engaging in power struggles, then Vampires won't find you very yummy.

What's the alternative to a power struggle, you may wonder? Well, it's to know what you really want, ask for it, and be willing to change your behavior to be more effective. For instance, your boss tells you to be punctual, but you have a day-care issue and always arrive ten minutes late. Your boss writes up a report and threatens you with suspension. You've now received your invitation to a power struggle. Do you RSVP and come in even later? What if you sat down with your boss and described your problem? What if you asked your boss his *reasons* for needing you to be on time? Maybe the phones open at 8 A.M. and no one can cover for you. If this is the case, you may need a job with more flexibility, or a different day care. Maybe your boss just has a policy and doesn't really need you at work by 8 A.M. sharp. In this case, your boss may value your technical skills and be willing to shave the ten minutes off your lunch hour. You won't ever find out if you act "normal" and join a power struggle by continuing to defy your boss by showing up late.

In corporate training seminars, I emphasize that to stop power struggles, you need to train people how to treat you and ask them to teach *you* how to treat them. Most people like the former part. They're less excited about changing their behavior to meet the needs of others. A lot of people start singing "I've gotta be me," even when I point out how they can increase their effectiveness by becoming more flexible in their behavior. They're afraid that if they change, they're giving in—or giving up.

Imagine that you wanted to talk to a woman who only spoke German, and you really wanted to influence her. But you didn't know German. I doubt that you'd insist she try to speak English. You'd probably be motivated to learn a little German to give yourself the power to communicate with her. You wouldn't confuse speaking her language with changing who you are.

Similarly, changing your words or behavior doesn't alter your soul. If you resist another person's ideas because you don't want to be controlled, you get to be right but you won't get what you want. "*Thy* will be done, not *my* will" is a helpful reminder because it points out that life isn't *just* about getting your way. If you get stubborn and insist that your way is the only way, you won't see other powerful options. If you can surrender your usual behavior and are open to what works better, you'll be pleasantly surprised by the results you can achieve.

Here's an example of how "I've gotta be me" fares as a response, compared to the more flexible language of Social Sorcery.

Your co-worker says: "When you talk to me as soon as I get into the office, I feel overwhelmed. I'd appreciate it if you'd wait until I get my coffee and can spend 30 minutes looking over my day and getting organized. Then I'll be ready to talk."

You ("I've gotta be me" response): "You don't understand that I have to talk with you first thing because my day gets so hectic. If you can't talk to me right away, then I don't have the information to do my job. Why can't you come in earlier?"

You (flexible response): "It sounds like having time first thing in the morning to get organized is very important to you [this is paraphrasing]. I'm wondering how I can get the information I need while still giving you time to settle in. Can we talk about some options?"

The Social Sorcery response is inflexible on *result,* but flexible on the *means* to get to the result. Paradoxically, the less you need to have power and control over others, the more powerful you become. One of the reasons "quality circles" and "teamwork programs" have worked better in Asia than in the United States is that Asian society strongly encourages interdependency. If we can give up being Lone Rangers and redefine strength, we can dramatically increase success in our relationships.

Picture skyscrapers and trees that are close to the ocean winds. The skyscrapers sway and the trees bend because the alternative is to break. Many species change genetically from one generation to the next in order to adapt. As Michael McGriffy, M.D., has said, "Blessed are the flexible, for they shall not be bent out of shape." Needing to be independent and do it your way means:

1. Confusing being powerful with being inflexible and refusing to alter your behavior to adapt to the needs of others.

2. Confusing being in control with having no needs. Having the inability to identify or the unwillingness to communicate what you want because you believe having needs is a weakness.

Think about how much time in your life you've wasted attempting to be right. Many arguments aren't about a pertinent issue but about whose self-esteem is going to win. If you focused instead on getting what you want, how much more effective could you be? If other people want or need to be right—let them. They can be right, and you can get what you want. You'll end up with the better part of the bargain.

When my clients are learning to escape power struggles, they have a tough time when someone thinks they're "wrong." They find it painful to be thought of in this way because they confuse being wrong with being bad. When you have the Interpersonal Edge, you'll discover that even when people make ridiculous demands, you'll get what you want if you don't argue about whether or not you're right.

For example, if I have a client who doesn't want to pay me for my services, I can easily agree that he has the right to work with someone else who doesn't mind not getting paid. I can let him know that what he wants is reasonable, and it's fine for him to find a professional that'll work with him pro bono. I, however, will expect timely payment from him. My client can tell me, "But Dr. Skube, you're *wrong*" till the cows come home. I realize that my client can believe that I'm *wrong,* but this doesn't make me *bad*. Nor does it make me wrong to expect what I expect. Because I don't argue about whether I'm right or not, my client *now* has to make a choice to work with me on my terms, or not at all. A power struggle about whether it's *right* for me to be paid can only occur if I try to defend my self-esteem.

When you stop playing the right/wrong game, you won't waste any more time on endless arguments. Even if you win and get to be right, you set up the game for another round. You never really win because next time you might have to be wrong. Instead, if you agree that the other person is right, but stand firm on what you want, you can focus on your end result and not on proving your point.

❖ O ❖

Knowing what we really want and asking for it is the hardest part of retiring from power struggles. I remember a client, Betty, who was angry when I didn't have her favorite Earl Grey tea in my waiting room. Betty thought she was telling me what she wanted—a bag of Earl Grey tea. Of course, depending on my shopping schedule, I might be out of that tea. I could have promised to stock huge quantities of Earl Grey so that I never ran out, but that would set her up to believe I would never disappoint her.

Instead, I asked Betty what it meant when I had her tea. She said it meant she was important to me. I asked her if there was any other way that she could find out if this were so. She admitted that she could ask me but that seemed pretty risky. I asked her if she tried to tell how other people felt about her based on whether they let her control them or not. She paused and confessed she did this with everyone. Betty had never considered that there was another way for her to check out her relationships, but she took the risk with me and stopped basing our relationship on tea leaves. Betty also stopped trying to control other people's behavior and started asking more directly for help and support from those around her.

Toddlers often get stuck in power struggles when they want their friends to play "their game." They'll exclaim, "You aren't my friend," if their buddy won't play what they want. Many adults get stuck in a similar toddler mind-set and don't realize that control is merely the consolation prize . . . not the brass ring. If you find that you're having toddler conversations with people, stop and figure out what you *really* want. If you know your end goal, you'll realize that there are as many ways to get what you want as there are ways to get to Rome.

Scripting: How to Ask for Money, Love, or Results

To escape power struggles, you have to give up the belief that if other people loved you they'd know what you want without your taking the risk to say it. Labeling other people "uncaring" because they lack telepathy can be temporarily satisfying, but it keeps you from seeing that you're actually afraid of rejection. Think back to a time when someone was upset with you but you didn't know why. I'll bet you can also remember a time you were upset with someone but were reluctant to tell the person what you wanted. You might find that you'd rather face a charging bull than ask for what you need because asking makes you feel vulnerable, needy, and dependent. However, if you clearly ask for what you want, you'll be able to spot those who can't, won't, or don't intend to give it to you. Vampires hate it when you speak up because they need control. If they met your needs, they'd have to retire from vampirism.

Lack of skill in articulating needs seems to particularly plague women. Men, in my practice, often complain that women simply won't tell them what they want. Even the great Sigmund Freud once exclaimed, "What do women want?" and it appears that he wasn't the only man to be confused. Women—yes, irrationally—seem to think that it's cheating to say specifically what they want. They'll express vague discontent, saying something like, "You don't love me."

In marriage or intimate relationships, women don't usually say, "On my birthday, I want dark chocolates, a quiet restaurant, and a foot rub." In the workplace, they won't typically admit, "I want to lead the Johnson project and be considered for vice president." When women tell men specifically what they want, men are often eager to do it—as long as they don't feel blamed. If a woman is dealing with a male Vampire, of course, it doesn't matter how *specifically* she communicates, she still won't get what she asks for.

Since telepathy is still a rare skill among the general public, I offer a tool I call *scripting* to make mind reading unnecessary. Scripting allows us to tell people what we need from them in a neutral, nonjudgmental manner. We all have recipes in life that work well for us. Unfortunately, we often don't let people know what ingredients make up our recipe. If we only like chocolate chip cookies without nuts, we'll get upset when someone hands us a chocolate chip cookie *with* walnuts. When this happens, we usually don't tell the person we don't like nuts, and munch unhappily on the cookie. Some people naturally have the same recipe as ours and we get along with them effortlessly. However, if we don't learn how to tell others what we need, we limit the number of people with whom we can have effective relationships.

Scripting works like this: The next time you have a problem with someone, imagine that you have a magic wand that you can wave to be transported into a perfect world with perfect people. What *specifically* could the other person do or say that would fix the problem? Even if the person isn't willing to act out your fantasy solution, at least you have a starting point to negotiate better.

For example, let's say your boss, Sarah, called you into her office and said, "Your performance has been disappointing, and I'm concerned about your attitude at work." Stop and imagine what you might say: "Sarah, when someone doesn't like what I'm doing, it helps if they tell me *specifically* what behavior they would like me to change. When you refer to my *performance* and *attitude,* I get confused because I'm not sure exactly what I've done."

As another example, let's say that you called your mother and were all excited because you stood up for yourself effectively at work. Your mother sighs and asks, "Why do you make everything so difficult?" Rather than hanging up in frustration, you could say, "Mom, what I really need to hear from you right now is that you're proud of me because you know that this was a hard thing for me to do." The beauty of scripting is that even if you don't get what you want, you know what it is, and are likely to feel you had a right to get it. You then have a better chance of getting it from *other* people, even if your mom hangs up. When you use *scripting,* in addition to being able to learn a new hobby or skill with the time you save in pouting, you'll notice the following benefits:

1. You'll feel less resentful when people do the "wrong" thing.

2. You'll feel more powerful and able to get what you want.

3. You'll actually get what you want more often.

4. You'll increase your effectiveness by increasing the support you get from others.

Toolkit for Scripting

Think of a situation where you're not getting what you want from someone. Imagine that you're watching the "Ideal World" channel on television. Ask the following questions:

1. "What would I like this person I'm having a problem with to be doing differently?" *Note:* Insisting they wouldn't create a problem in the first place won't help you. Remember, you're getting ready to coach them. A good coach doesn't look at a player and bark, "Stop being yourself!"

2. "What would this person be saying differently to me?"

3. "What emotional needs do I have that I haven't articulated to myself or to the other person?" (For instance, you're worried, angry, or want approval. Remember, you don't have to confess all of your feelings, but you do need to know what they are.)

Then take action by:

4. Calling up a friend of yours and practicing scripting. Have them role-play the real person you'd like to have the scripting conversation with.

5. When you feel confident enough, call up the *real* person and use scripting.

An Example of Scripting

Giselle was feeling ignored by her husband and dreaded the upcoming Valentine's Day because she was anticipating disappointment. When she used scripting, she imagined what he'd do and say if he were the "perfect" husband. That night after the kids were in bed, she said, "Honey, for Valentine's Day I'd like you to arrange a babysitter, then call me up and ask for a date. Then I'd like you to meet me at our front door with a bouquet of red roses, and take me to a candlelit restaurant I've never been to before." Giselle almost fell off the couch when her husband's face broke into a wide smile and he said, "I love it when I don't have to guess what you want!"

You can also use scripting in combination with the "I" language you learned in the chapter on Word Wizardry. Use the word "I" at the beginning, describe the other person's actions or words, and end by scripting exactly you want:

I noticed when you said _____ *and did* _____, *I reacted by* [fill in your emotional reaction].

Next, tell the person your script for what you'd like instead: *I know you can't read my mind, and what would work better with me is if you would* [fill in what you'd like them to say instead and do instead].

For example, if you're angry because your spouse doesn't help with housework you might say: *I noticed when you said* **you were going to watch football** *and* **sat down on the couch,** *I reacted by deciding you think the housework is totally my responsibility.*

You can then script what you'd like instead from your spouse: *I know you can't read my mind, and what would work better for me is if you would* **ask me if you can help me with anything around the house before you sit down to watch the game.**

Now the two of you can negotiate how to best solve the problem. You've just communicated to the other person your specific recipe for relating effectively.

Many of my executive-coaching clients say they're afraid to tell people what they want because they feel obligated to protect the other person's feelings. You only have the illusion of power if you believe that you can control people's emotional responses by withholding data. When you don't tell them what you want, they don't have the information they need to respond appropriately. In the long run, this creates bigger messes than telling the truth in the first place. For example, you want your assistant to quit making errors, but you don't want to hurt his feelings, so you say nothing and keep covering for him. You feel more and more resentful until you impulsively fire him. He sues you and wins because nothing was documented indicating that there was a problem.

When you censor your requests to people, you can count on your communication with them becoming confusing and difficult. If, for instance, you think your boss is favoring another employee, you might not bring it up because the only way you know how to talk about it is to accuse your boss of being unfair. You know that this won't work so you don't say anything and marinate in your frustration. Your sarcastic remarks increase, and your boss knows that something is wrong. He guesses that you're mad because you didn't get a larger raise. He doesn't confront you because the only way he can think of talk to you is to accuse you of being ungrateful. Thus, neither of you air out your true differences because both of you don't know *how* to talk in a way where you each take responsibility for your feelings, observations, and needs.

Instead, if you had simply scripted your request to your boss, you might have said, "I'd like to be sent to two sales trainings this year to learn new skills." Now, you might get turned down, but at least you'd have a shot at getting what you want. If you keep getting turned down, rather than continuing your previous vague, blaming complaints about him playing favorites, you can talk to him about your need for more training.

The Inner Predator

An inner version of the Vampire can be found in our inside voices that torture us with criticism, doubt, or self-hatred. Freud described these inner demons as one of two motivations driving human behavior: Libido (drive toward life) and Thanatos (drive toward death). These inner demons kill off our aliveness and keep us numb. To the extent that these parts of us are running our lives, we may be self-destructive, addicted, or undermining ourselves.

The inner predator is most apparent in dreams. When my clients dream of serial killers or scary monsters, they may fear that they're losing their mind. The truth is that they're finding in their dream characters the part of their mind where the inner predator lives. We may dream of insane women chasing us with knives, literal demons, or vicious animals. When my clients work with these dream images, they find angry, needy, scared, or sad parts of themselves. As they see the connections between the inner predators and their unacknowledged feelings, the dream characters are either killed off or transformed into allies.

I remember a repeated dream I had about a huge monster chasing me. I kept waking up each morning drenched in sweat and exhausted from "running." Before I went to sleep one night I decided that if I had the nightmare again, I'd make a conscious effort to confront it rather than run away. That night when I had my monster dream again, it took every ounce of courage I had to stop running, turn around, and confront the monster with, "What do you want from me?" The monster suddenly shrank to my size, started to cry, and said, "I'm lonely." When I woke up and thought about my dream, I realized that I *was* too isolated and made efforts to be with my friends more. The huge monster never came back to haunt me. I've also had dreams in which I killed the image and it didn't return.

Think of the inner predator as the part of us that gets damaged in childhood and grows in a twisted fashion. These monsters often have useful purposes when we're children, especially if we're in abusive homes. In crazy childhood homes, an inner predator may help us deny that our dad is sexually molesting our sister, or make us obsessive rather than anxious, or keep us from crying when we get beat up. None of these reactions represent healthy *adult* behavior, but seemingly insane reactions are a good solution when you're a kid in a nutty environment. The problem occurs when we leave home and take our predators with us. Denial, inability to notice anxiety, and numbing ourselves don't work so well in the outside world. We become addicts, workaholics, or stay stoic and don't see the inner predator sucking our vitality.

Toolkit for the Inner Predator

Do you remember the mythology about how a Vampire can't come into your home unless you invite it over your threshold? Similarly, damaging people have less ability to harm you if you don't invite them in via your inner predator. To identify your inner predator ask the following questions:

1. What type of people do I get hurt by?

2. What are the common themes among these people (for example, they frequently use me)?

3. Is there any internal voice that agrees that I can't set limits or say no?

4. Pay attention to your nightmares. Describe your inner demons. Do they have anything in common with the people who hurt me?

5. How can I be more aware when I'm dealing with these types of people so that I spot them early on and don't invite them into my life?

An Example of the Inner Predator

Bart always seemed to get into relationships with girlfriends, co-workers, and friends who were verbally abusive. He prided himself on being soft-spoken, rational, and forgiving. He also had a recurring dream about an evil witch who chased him through a forest. He suffered from migraines that his doctor said were caused by "stress." While using this tool, Bart saw that his inability to access his anger made him invite abusive people into his life. He could see that he needed to "blow his top" when necessary, and set clear-cut boundaries that he stuck to. He started to balance his forgiving nature with appropriate assertiveness. Within a short time, his headaches were gone, his nightmare had ceased, he no longer chose verbally abusive people to associate with, and the "sometimes difficult" people who remained in his life treated him with a new level of respect.

As you disengage from power struggles and learn to script what you want, Vampires won't find you delicious, and your inner predator won't undermine you. The next chapter helps you spot the most common types of impossible people so you can protect yourself and exit gracefully from a situation before getting wounded.

CHAPTER 11

GAMES VAMPIRES PLAY

"An effective way to deal with predators is to taste terrible."
— Unknown

In a society where winning through intimidation is actually considered a reasonable strategy, you'll notice that some people will feel as if you're trying to control them, no matter how specific and non-accusatory your language is. If you practice and use the tools in this book, these individuals will find you more trouble than you're worth and eventually leave you alone. But you can speed up the process if you can recognize the most popular and common ploys they use.

Vampire Power Plays

People who operate like Vampires venerate fear not love, and are the acid test of Social Sorcery. Tools that are effective on those who want love don't work on predators because they want control, not affection or consciousness. You'll have to accept that no amount of magic can turn a Vampire into an angel. Extremely difficult people will make it impossible to have the type of conversation that's necessary to work out conflict. Instead, they'll blame you, gossip about you, and do whatever they can to damage you, even from a distance. Basically, they aren't capable of engaging in a give-*and*-take dialogue.

Predators will make sure they do the taking—thank you very much—and that *you* do the giving. You'll need to have the basics of Social Sorcery mastered before you can easily handle a truly difficult person. Dealing with Vampires is like taking a graduate course in Social Sorcery. They'll show you both what you still need to practice, and how far you've come with your skills.

There are many books that outline and label categories of difficult people. These works can be fun to read because there's something emotionally satisfying about categorizing the rotten behavior of predators in our lives. Unfortunately, few if any of these books give you the specialized skills to neutralize problem personalities. Merely identifying these people can actually play into a sense of powerlessness that we all experience when we don't know what to do. The next section of this chapter goes beyond identifying traits of problem individuals. It tells you *how* to protect yourself.

Power Play #1:
It's Your Problem if You Feel Bad When I Hit You

Some folks abide by the idea that you "have to take personal responsibility" for your feelings while they avoid responsibility for *their* behavior. The tactic these people use works like this: When someone complains to an abusive person about a behavior, the predator calmly replies, "Well, I can't help it if you feel that way. It's your own fault, because I can't *make* you feel anything."

Many people have been stumped by this clever reply because there *is some* logic to it. While it's true that others aren't responsible for our feelings, they *are* accountable for the quality of the relationship they create between themselves and us. Let's look at a protective response to this power play, with the example of an aggressive co-worker who keeps delegating work to your employees:

You: "Andrew, I feel uncomfortable when you go directly to my employees and give them assignments without letting me know what you're asking them to do."

Andrew: "Well, that's your problem. I'm not responsible for your feelings."

You: "Andrew, are you saying you're not interested in working out this problem with me?" (*Note:* This is paraphrasing.)

Andrew: "Well, it *is* your problem. I didn't make you uncomfortable. If you choose to be uncomfortable, there's nothing I can do."

You: "So, are you saying you're not willing to talk to me about directly assigning work to my employees without letting me know? I'd like to work this out without going to our boss, but if you're unwilling to talk to me, I'll have to turn this problem over to her." (*Note:* This uses both Tele-visioning and paraphrasing.)

Paraphrasing and Tele-visioning can be very helpful in flushing out a difficult person's motives. With this kind of power play, focus on the person's *behavior*. Don't allow them to make your *feelings* the issue. Use lots of paraphrasing to hold them accountable for their actions. And keep in mind that these people respond to power, not love. If you don't set a consequence that can negatively impact them, they won't respond to your request for change.

Toolkit for Power Play #1

Let's say that Fred, one of your employees, has been showing up late and coming to work with whiskey on his breath. When you confront him with this, Fred says, "I don't know what you're talking about. You're always picking on me and trying to find something wrong with what I'm doing. You're always so demanding and critical, always trying to hurt my feelings. You never did like me. Why don't you mellow out and give me a break? Then maybe our relationship will work."

To focus the issue on the other person's behavior and not let them turn it into *your* problem, you might say, "Fred, it sounds as if you want to talk about how I pick on you and am mean to you. But right now I'm interested in staying focused on your consistent lateness and the alcohol I keep smelling on your breath. If you and I can't find an immediate solution, I'll have to turn this over to Human Resources."

Power Play #2: Petty Tyrants

You probably know better than to argue with junkyard dogs, but do you know how to recognize their human equivalents? With a Petty Tyrant, you'll find that any sincere attempt at communication is as useless as arguing with a growling canine. Historically, a tyrant was someone who had life-and-death power over other people, but they're also alive and well in modern times. Only now they don't have real life-and-death power over you—they just *try* to get you to *think* they do.

There are two ways of approaching relationships: mutual power and power over. The communication techniques described in this book work with people who are interested in mutual power. Petty Tyrants surprise us because they're willing to lose business, relationships, or money rather than lose control and power over others.

The only force a tyrant responds to is whatever punitive power you can muster: legal guidelines, corporate policies, or friends in high places. What won't work is trying to create win-win solutions. The Petty Tyrant's idea of a win-win solution is they win and they win (and you lose—*totally*). Using communication techniques on a Petty Tyrant might remind you of the saying, "Don't try to teach a pig to sing. It exhausts you and annoys the hell out of the pig."

Petty Tyrants are easy to recognize by their total disregard for the rules of social life, often to the point of self-destruction. I once worked with a CEO, Joseph, who had many business relationships within another company that had a Petty Tyrant president. I was able to help Joseph see that this executive was a predator. Joseph and I watched as this president ruined his professional reputation, alienated his customer base, and eventually went bankrupt. Working together, Joseph and I used the Interpersonal Edge toolkits and minimized his engagement with the tyrant and his company. As a result, Joseph's organization was protected as the other company went under.

Most people find it amazing that anyone would ruin their own business in an attempt to stay in control. However, for a Petty Tyrant, life isn't about *winning;* it's about wielding *power* over other people, no matter what the cost or consequences.

Petty Tyrants are masters of the short-term solution. As long as they can stay in control, they're not particularly concerned about the future. Fortunately, Petty Tyrants make up a very small percentage of the population. The important thing is to identify these "control freaks" early and cut your losses before you lose your shirt trying to make the relationship work.

Power Play #3: The Sniper

Snipers treat communication as if it's guerrilla warfare. They seem to hide under bushes, around corners, and underground, popping up only long enough to shoot you verbally before they go back into hiding. Snipers never confront you directly with their feelings because getting mad *in a direct way* is too threatening to them. They're generally angry people who are looking for someone to vent at, and you'll do quite nicely. Snipers make it hard to address a particular issue. They may tell you that while *they* don't have a problem with you, "other people" don't like you or what you're doing. Snipers will imply that *they're* doing you a favor by telling you, and *you* should be grateful.

Please don't buy into this reasoning. No one *ever* communicates negative secondhand information without a self-serving motive for doing so.

Snipers are masters at the art of vague communication, so you can use Tele-visioning to force them to be more specific. Snipers like to use vague complaints about us—it's their favorite ammunition. If you use Tele-visioning, you'll insist that the Sniper tell you *exactly* what you've done and you'll be talking *specifically* to the Sniper about what you want. Your language will be clear enough so that both of you can *see* what you're talking about as if on a TV screen. In addition to Tele-visioning, the following guidelines will shield you when you're dealing with a Sniper.

1. Don't let curiosity kill your cat. All of us wonder what other people think about us. We hope people like us, and are concerned about what people say behind our backs. The Sniper will use this curiosity against you. Keep in mind that Snipers distort what others say, or put words in other people's mouths. Then the Sniper can insult you and criticize you about an issue without taking responsibility. Don't let them get away with it! As soon as the Sniper says, "Well, you know John seems to be upset with you . . ." tell the Sniper, "Please stop." Then say firmly and clearly, "I'm not interested in what *John* thinks unless *John* wants to tell me."

The Sniper may even try telling you what "other people" think without identifying names. This puts you in a bind where you can't confront the Sniper (after all, it isn't their opinion), and you can't confront the *other people* because they didn't tell you directly. Realize that Snipers are not above putting words in other people's mouths or distorting what was really said about you.

2. If a Sniper tries to tell you what other people think, question him or her, saying something like, "Bob, I'm puzzled about why you told me this, and I'm wondering if you might have the same issue with me." Snipers will immediately deny the possibility, but they now know that you're aware of their real motives. Finish up by saying, "I know that you're just trying to help me, but in the future, please don't tell me what others think. Besides, I'm terrible at keeping secrets, and if you tell me what someone has said, I'm very likely to go to the person and let them know you were concerned about their opinion of me."

You can also tell the Sniper, "When you tell me other people think poorly of me, it hurts my feelings, and I know you wouldn't want to *purposely* do that."

These strategies make it impossible for the Sniper to express their anger in an indirect manner. Since you won't tolerate indirect hostility anymore, and Snipers won't discuss being angry at you directly, they'll need to find someone else to snipe at. During the decades I've worked as a corporate consultant, I've learned to pay attention to how much gossip goes on in a company. This is a good indicator of organizational health, because extensive gossip requires a network of people willing to engage in the vigorous, indirect, and angry communication that breeds sniping.

Power Play #4: The Expert

Experts act like they're friends with God, leap tall buildings at a single bound, and work minor miracles in spare moments. In reality, the Expert's power play is the easiest to manage. They're merely insecure people who are afraid that you're going to see how vulnerable they are. Most of us will attempt to attack Experts or try to prove them wrong, but this makes them all the more defensive. The best way to deal with an Expert is use your listening skills, paraphrase, and honor his or her knowledge. Then use "I" language to talk about your own experience.

For example, let's say you're dealing with an Expert who thinks she knows the best way to do the annual budget for your department. Instead of criticizing the approach she's using, try something like: "Mary, when I was in charge of putting my budget together with our finance committee, I found talking to several committee members really helpful—particularly, Frank, Rachel, and Sally, and they suggested that . . ."

In other words, don't focus on *why* an Expert is wrong. Focus on *what* you know and *how* you know it. If the Expert wants to argue with you, gracefully decline by saying, "Well it sounds like my approach might not be what you need." If the Expert is an employee you need to supervise, focus on your desired end result. If the employee argues, simply say, "Well, it sounds like my idea may not work for you, *and* we need to get this done. Why don't you see if you can come up with another way to do it and get back to me?"

When dealing with Experts, expect issues related to inadequacy and insecurity to arise for you. You'll be sorely tempted to engage in a power struggle to prove that *you* know more than the Expert. Remind yourself when you communicate with this type of person that you're knowledgeable and well intentioned. It's hard for people to get your goat if you don't offer it to them. Instead, if you let the Expert have nearly superhero authority, they'll usually be glad to give you whatever you want.

The next two power plays are personality disorders described in the diagnostic manual for therapists. Even professional counselors may have trouble working with these next two types. One of the best ways to spot them is to notice when you start feeling absolutely crazy when you're dealing with someone.

Most of us don't realize that there are three main categories of mental health: normal neurosis (most of us fall into this one); personality disorders; and the most serious, psychosis (this is where someone believes they're Jesus Christ or is otherwise delusional). Psychotics are the easiest to spot because their version of reality is *clearly* different from most people.

People with personality disorders appear normal—at first. They're not ill enough to be psychotic, but their version of reality is profoundly different from normal neurotics. When someone starts to act strangely, most of us aren't aware that there's a category of mental health between normal and psychotic. I've watched as my clients torture themselves trying to make sense of the odd behavior of someone with a personality disorder. If you recognize the following traits in someone, you're not dealing with a normal neurotic. Be aware of, and prepared for, the fact that these people have *severe* emotional problems. Don't expect them to follow or respond to normal social rules.

Power Play #5:
I'm the Only One Who Matters (Narcissists)

The first personality-disorder group, Narcissists, act like they're the only people in the universe and everyone else is on the planet to serve them. Characteristics of Narcissists include: an extreme lack of empathy, and a strong negative reaction and sensitivity to criticism (even if you didn't mean to criticize). Narcissists exploit others, think they're more important than everyone else, and feel that they deserve to be treated in special ways. They believe that their problems are unique; and are obsessed with fantasies of perfect success, love, or power. They have a sense of entitlement, require constant attention, and are very envious of others.

Although Narcissists act as if they think highly of themselves, they actually lack self-esteem, struggle with intense shame, and see other people as a way of filling the void inside of them.

Narcissists are psychologically handicapped when it comes to seeing the needs of others. Sometimes my friends will humorously let me know they want attention by saying, "Well, enough about you!" Normal neurotics may joke about being self-centered, but Narcissists see no humor in their self-absorption. They also have trouble getting help from therapy because they usually regard the therapist as being too critical, and then bolt.

I remember a client who had a Narcissistic personality disorder and came to me because of her chronic conflicts with family members and friends. Whenever I tried to point out ways in which she'd contributed to her problems, she became very angry. I finally said, "Do you simply want me to tell you that your problems are caused because other people aren't giving you enough?" She nodded enthusiastically. I told her that I couldn't help her without focusing on changes she could make. She didn't return for another session.

If you have to deal with Narcissists, try the following:

1. Be neutral and nonjudgmental in your choice of words. Use language that focuses on positive attributes. If you want a Narcissistic employee to make more sales, you might say, "John, you have an amazing ability to find customers and sell them our product. Because of that, I'll bet that your numbers will keep going up each month. I don't know what I'd do without you!"

2. Always let a Narcissist save face, even if it means crafting excuses for their behavior. If your mother-in-law just screamed at your kids, you might say, "Martha, I know that you love the kids and that you're under unusual pressure today. Normally, you'd never raise your voice to your grandkids. Can you please use a softer voice?

3. If you have a problem with a Narcissist, make sure that you describe the problem in a way that focuses on behavior, don't attack their personality, and use Tele-visioning.

4. Anticipate that these people will frequently accuse you of attacking them and not meeting their needs.

5. Since Narcissists don't easily respect boundaries, set your limits firmly and repetitively, and enforce them.

For instance, if you're dealing with a Narcissistic boss, a conversation where you have the Interpersonal Edge might go like this:

You: "My wife has been diagnosed with cancer and needs to go into the hospital for surgery. I need to schedule a week of vacation time so I can stay home with her while she recuperates. We can schedule the surgery anytime in the next two months."

Boss: "You know that we're under enormous pressure from our management team to institute this new marketing campaign. I need you to be here for the next two months. You'll just need to find a nurse to stay with your wife."

You: "Finding a nurse for my wife after her surgery isn't an option for me. I realize that that it's inconvenient timing, and I appreciate that it will create a hardship for you that I'll be gone for a week, but which week would be best for me to take off in the next two months?"

Boss: "You're putting me in a terrible position. I can't believe that you're asking me for a week right now!"

You: "Again, I know that it's terrible timing. My other option is to go to Human Resources and ask for family leave. It's not an option for me to leave my wife with a nurse."

Boss: "Fine! It appears that you put your personal life in front of your career. Take next week." (The boss then shoots you an icy look, but you did get your time off so that you could take care of your priorities.)

Don't ever expect a Narcissist to be empathetic, care about your needs, or see your problems. If you have to deal with them, then appeal to *their* needs, be complimentary, and never hint at their imperfections. Most of us will find that doing so constantly gets exhausting, so it's fine to carefully evaluate whether what you're getting out of the relationship is worth the price. If you stop cater-ing to a Narcissist's needs, anticipate rage or icy indifference.

Power Play #6:
I Need You; I Hate You (Borderlines)

Borderlines are hard people to manage. Many private-practice therapists screen Borderlines out of their practice because they take so much time and emotional energy (even when the relationship is limited to one session a week). If you have a relationship with a Borderline, you've probably become used to feeling crazy, inad-equate, and furious. And you may even think that it's your fault. Borderlines are usually narcissistic as well, so they also possess the traits described in Power Play #5. In addition, they're overwhelm-ingly needy and vacillate between hating and worshiping people. Being in a relationship with them is similar emotionally to having someone threaten to die if you leave, while alternately clinging to or hitting you. Borderlines have a lot of terror and chaos going on inside of them. They try to deal with their anxiety and rage by stuffing their feelings into their relationships with others. The more intimate you are with a Borderline, the worse their behavior gets.

The characteristics of Borderlines include: unstable and intense personal relationships where they either idealize or hate the other person; highly impulsive behavior such as sexual addiction, sub-stance abuse, or binge eating; rapid mood shifts (one minute the person is elated, the next feeling suicidal); and inappropriate, in-tense, out-of-control anger. A Borderline's uncertainty about their true self shows up in confusion about career, sexual orientation, type of friends, or values. They have a chronic feeling of emptiness or boredom, and make frantic attempts to avoid abandonment.

If there's a Borderline in your life, know that the tools you're about to learn will minimize the damage these people can create, but it's normal to find them very frustrating. When dealing with these types, use lots of paraphrasing, and keep the conversation focused on their feelings and thoughts. Don't let them blame their feelings, actions, or reactions on you.

If you were the wife of a Borderline, a typical conversation where you stay focused on your husband's feelings might go like this:

Borderline: "I think that you should dress differently. Why can't you dress sexier? And, you know, your feet are really big. They're not very pretty. By the way, I'm tired of your criticism about my drinking."

Response: "It sounds like you have lots of issues about how people in your life dress, and you're nervous about your drinking."

Borderline: "They're not *my* issues; it's *you* that's the problem. Besides, you're always criticizing me. A good wife never criticizes her husband. Your job is to make me feel good."

Response: "So what you're saying is that you think the job of a wife is to never say she's unhappy with her husband's behavior, right?"

Borderline: "Well, what would you know about being a good wife? I treat you so well and all you do is criticize me. You know lots of women would want to be married to a man like me. Besides, I'm not sure I love you anymore. Women are so impossible. I think a man would be easier to be married to."

Many Borderlines are very intelligent. If you try to reason with them, they'll blame you, and come up with seemingly logical reasons why it's your fault. In the last example, even if the wife dressed differently, could change the size of her feet, stopped expressing unhappiness, or became a man, it wouldn't improve the relationship. The Borderline would just invent a new series of complaints. The way to avoid ending up in a little white outfit at the psychiatric unit when dealing with a Borderline is to do the following:

1. Expect that a Borderline will bring up any inadequacies you have.

2. Refuse to get dragged into debates about *their* perceptions of *your* inadequacies.

3. Establish ironclad boundaries around your time, what you'll accept, and what you want, and get any business deals on paper in detailed legal language.

4. Expect that the Borderline won't respect you, your time, or any agreements you make and will constantly test any boundary you set.

5. Use paraphrasing to keep yourself sane and the Borderline accountable.

As you review this chapter's list of power plays, you may feel discouraged, and wish that you could live on a planet with nicer people. Take heart, because although you can't avoid difficult individuals, in the final three chapters of this book I'll show you how these people can actually contribute to your growth. If you have difficult people in your life right now, be comforted by the knowledge that their behavior isn't your fault. And although relationships with them can feel as if they're sucking the life out of you, they aren't necessarily "bad."

In myths, vampires are created by other vampires. As kids, many difficult people have had repeated exposure to abusive, vampirelike people. Some children are resilient, get helped by someone, or get therapy early and escape becoming a predator. Other kids grow up to become monsters themselves. You didn't break these people, and you won't fix them. But you *can* use the powerful toolkits of Social Sorcery. When you have the Interpersonal

Edge, you won't end up losing blood when a predatory person's behavior turns ugly.

Vampire Enablers

Now that you've developed radar for difficult people, you'll also need it for a class of people I call "Vampire Enablers." These folks enable difficult people to suck the life out of everyone else. In 12-step literature, there's lots of discussion about "enabling" addiction, which refers to people who are connected to addicts and help them engage in their addiction (alcohol, drugs, food, sex, gambling, shopping, and so on).

In vampire mythology, there are actually enablers of the undead who are called "ghouls." These are mortals who drink vampire blood and become bound to the vampire. Ghouls help vampires prey on humans in the hopes that one day the vampire will honor them by letting them become one of the undead.

Vampire Enablers, in real life, act at lot like ghouls because they hope that by being "helpful" to destructive people they'll gain comfort and avoid anxiety. Enablers also resemble ghouls because they help unhealthy people damage others—for example, parents who give alcoholic adult children money to buy cars, or those who know someone else's child is being abused but don't want to make the parents of the child upset by reporting the abuse. These people may claim they're being "helpful," but clearly, "helpfulness" is not a good trait in all circumstances.

In many ways, Vampire Enablers are well-meaning people who have an amazing ability to deny the truth. Enablers tend to believe that corporations are always ethical, government is always fair, and sexual abuse doesn't happen in good neighborhoods.

You can see a dreadful large-scale example of Vampire Enabler "helpfulness" when you consider the unimaginable atrocities done to the Jewish people during Hitler's reign. It might be comforting to believe that this global example of how badly we can treat each other was the result of a small group of evil people. Unfortunately, psychologists such as Alice Miller have pointed out the ways in which Hitler appealed to the German masses—not just his inner circle. The majority of well-meaning Germans who looked the other way, denied the horror of the death camps, or blamed the Jewish people supported one of the darkest chapters in human history. No one can undo the damage, but we can, hopefully, learn how such inhumanity occurs so that no group of people *ever again* experiences such inhumane treatment.

Vampire Enablers will blame you when a predatory person attacks you. They'll say that *you* must have done something to *deserve* the Vampire's bite. They figure that evil is something that happens to *other* people who deserve it, not to "helpful" people like them. This type of rationalization comforts the Vampire Enablers until they believe that they're magically safe from malevolence.

Enablers find acknowledging evil to be too messy, too inconvenient, and frankly, anxiety inducing. It's much better to paint the world with Disney-style rainbows where every villain gets transformed and love reigns supreme. It's much easier to live in a world where the comfort of denying evil can be chosen over the truth that evil exists. Vampire Enablers don't realize that the best protection against malevolence is to see it coming—not to pretend a scorpion is a cute, loving pet that's just misunderstood.

Enablers superstitiously believe that "being nice" will keep them safe from evil: "If I pet the bad doggie gently, I bet it won't bite me." Unfortunately, bad doggies seldom cooperate with this deal. Ironically, the people Vampires prey upon the most, in the long run, are their own Vampire Enablers. After all they're close, available, and innocently looking the other way. Some Enablers do buy time while appeasing the Vampire, but they just end up being the last one the Vampire has for lunch.

It won't always make you popular to stand up and declare out loud, "If it walks like a Vampire, talks like a Vampire, and sucks blood like a Vampire—it probably *is* a Vampire." Vampire Enablers will just sing you their favorite song, "Can't we all just get along?" This is a nice little ditty . . . if you're not dealing with a predator. Predators don't *want* to get along; they want *power*. Unless you're prepared to sacrifice your peace of mind, integrity, and anything else the Vampire wants, you're *not* going to get along.

When dealing with Vampire Enablers, stay away from the Vampire while the Enablers get cozy with their friend. If getting hurt personally doesn't convince Enablers that they're dealing with a Vampire, then they're headed toward becoming a predator themselves. The more distance you put between yourself and Enablers in denial, the better off you'll be because they'll expose you and themselves to repeated abuse. If a Vampire Enabler does embrace the truth, he or she can be a powerful ally. In myths, vampires need fresh blood to survive. If people stop denying that evil exists and make it impossible for human Vampires to get new blood, Vampires are forced to find easier feeding grounds or starve.

The lack of courage of Vampire Enablers and their refusal to see evil can be thoroughly annoying. When an Enabler in your life is being "helpful" to a Vampire, you may find Dante Alighieri's quote comforting: "The hottest places in hell are reserved for those who, in a period of moral crisis, maintain their neutrality."

∴ ☉ ∴

Most of us have moments when we're tempted to look the other way when a predatory person is on the loose. Reflect on how you usually respond when you see someone intentionally hurting another. Do you generally figure that the person deserves it because of something he or she did? Do you believe that the person doing the hurting wouldn't do that to *you* because *you* wouldn't deserve it? Do you think that being nice will protect *you* from being hurt? If the abuser has something you want, such as acceptance, status, or influence, do you use this as an excuse to look the other way? If so, that's the perfect direction to be looking so that the Vampire can have access your neck.

If you've discovered that sometimes *you're* an Enabler, realize that being "helpful" to abusive people supports evil in *your* life. Your ability to see abuse and spot predators will allow you to steer clear of damaging situations. You'll also be able to develop support networks of people who will protect you. As predators in your life get starved for victims, you'll find they move away, move on, and move over so you can have relationships built on affection not fear.

Think of the power we'd have to improve the world if, collectively, we stopped ignoring abuse and refused to aid predators.

People will treat you in the same way they treat others. If you know people who are diplomatic, patient, or generous, they'll be this way with you not necessarily because you deserve it, but because that's how they operate. If you know people who *only* want power and you see them hurt others—you've received your first warning. See the predator coming your way and protect yourself.

Now that you know how to deal with Vampires and their Enablers, and have a good idea how to manage your inner demons, let's find out how to create cooperative relationships with the rest of the souls on the planet.

CHAPTER 12

CREATING COOPERATION

"Hell is—other people."
— Jean-Paul Sartre

And They Lived Happily Ever After . . .

I've always figured that fairy tales end just before the hard part because conflict is as popular a topic as warts. We usually want to avoid it. It isn't polite dinner conversation, so we pretend we don't have it. We'd mostly rather read about losing weight than losing arguments. Besides, avoiding high-calorie food seems easier than resolving differences.

Hopelessness and lack of information about conflict can fuel our aversion. Few people jump out of bed in the morning thinking, *Oh goody! I get to create cooperation today!* Mostly we get gloomy when confronted with a disagreement and think about all the ways in which it can go wrong.

If we don't know how to work through differences, however, our professional and personal lives can feel as if we're walking through a minefield. There's no gene that we know of for resolving conflict, although a lucky few of us did come from families that modeled fighting fair. However, more of us came from backgrounds where "no one fought" (translation: no one worked anything out). Then there are the families where people hit, screamed, or had tantrums (and I'm talking about the grown-ups).

Where couples are concerned, research tells us that the strongest indicator of a successful marriage isn't being in love, having great sex, or amazing chemistry, but the ability to fight well. The current divorce rate would imply that most of us don't possess these skills or even know that they're *necessary* in order to stay married. The alternative to learning to fight fair is to limit yourself to a small corner of the world where everyone agrees with you. But in reality, only the dead are conflict free (and we can't even be *sure* about that).

The living will find that the biggest stumbling blocks to working through disagreements are the fairy tales regarding conflict. For instance, most people believe that good relationships shouldn't be conflicted. When a difference of opinion becomes obvious, most folks will figure the *other* person must be *bad* because disagreements *shouldn't* occur. People then withdraw or attack, and decide the relationship is *totaled*. Well, we don't declare a car totaled when a tire goes flat. We anticipate that vehicles will need repairs, and we fix them. Unfortunately, most of us don't anticipate that relationships will naturally break, too. Thus, we often declare them totaled without seeing the option of repair. Some other popular conflict myths include:

Myth #1: *If I avoid it, it will go away.*

Reality: If you avoid it, the conflict will get worse and be harder to resolve. The best time to work on a conflict is when it first becomes apparent. Most people wait until a big explosion occurs before they work through an issue. The more time that passes before a negotiation starts, the more resentment builds. Strong, built-up emotions make it difficult to discuss or resolve issues.

For instance, let's say that one of your co-workers is always late with his assignments and you have to pick up the slack. First you try hinting, then you try humor, and finally you try letting the project go to pieces. Your co-worker just continues to be late and your resentment grows. One day your boss asks you how the project's going. You blow up and bark, "I'm sick of all the pressure! Joe never gets his work done, and no one seems to notice that I always have to fill in for him!" Then you stomp out. Obviously, you haven't earned points with your boss, and *you're* the one who looks bad, not Joe. If you'd dealt with Joe early on, this scene wouldn't have happened.

Myth #2: *If I talk about it, it will get worse.*
Reality: If you talk about it without applying conflict-resolution skills, you may make the situation worse. However, it's *guaranteed* to get worse if you don't do *anything*. Just by discussing the issues, each person will walk away with a better understanding of their differences. If you have the Interpersonal Edge, then you communicate well, and your chances of *improving* the situation are high.

Myth #3: *It really isn't that bad (or maybe I'm imagining it).*
Reality: If it isn't that bad, why are you thinking about it all the time? Consider how much time you've wasted *not* addressing the problem. Besides, if it *really* isn't that bad, it will get better, faster, once it's discussed.

Myth #4: *It will take too much time to resolve the problem.*
Reality: By not resolving the problem, you're keeping it around until it becomes the elephant in the living room you constantly bump into. Talking about a disagreement takes time up front, but it saves a lot more in the long run.

Myth #5: *I'll get a reputation as a troublemaker.*
Reality: A lack of interpersonal skills is cited in organizational research as the most common reason professionals get derailed from promotional tracks. People who readily resolve conflicts, on

the other hand, are a gold mine for business because they're so rare. If you want to seriously improve your reputation professionally, learn to work out differences with co-workers, customers, and supervisors.

On the home front, one of the most common reasons why couples split up is an inability to negotiate. Research shows that after each divorce, the likelihood of another one increases dramatically. After a relationship fails, people often don't realize they need to learn better conflict-resolution skills. Then they usually end up marrying a similar type of spouse in a new body and have the *same* fights with the *same* results.

Connecting in the Heat of Battle

In the days of the Old West, a difference of opinion was resolved easily—with a bullet. Resolving a difference by annihilating your opponent was a win/lose negotiation model. If you won, you got to feel triumphant—until someone tried to get even. After all, it wasn't unusual for a vengeful relative of the dead guy to pick up a gun and go after the victor.

Most people start to drown when they get into a conflict because they have no model for navigating the disagreement. In my corporate-training sessions, I give clients a handout they can use as a map for handling any future issues. The handout contains the following easy-to-remember, two-step model and four-step process. Many of my clients tell me that they find this information so helpful that they post it in their office at work or on their bulletin board at home to use when dealing with disagreements that occur on the phone, via e-mail, or prior to what they think will be a tough discussion.

Since most people are more than a little annoyed when they start conflict resolutions, I call the two-step model **ROAR (Real Outcome/Affirm Relationship)**. I'll now show you the **ROAR** process and then give you examples of how to apply it.

1. **Real Outcome:** Ask these questions of the other person and yourself: "Why do you want what you want?" or "How would it be helpful if you got that?" Then suggest ideas that incorporate both of your real outcomes. (*Hint:* What people say they want initially is *rarely* their real outcome.)

2. **Affirm Relationship:** Don't lie, but *do* mention whatever is positive about the relationship. If you stay focused on a solution and let the other person maintain their self-esteem, they'll *want* to help you. It might be "I care about this relationship" or "It's important to me that we work well together." Use the following guidelines:

   - Set a mutually agreeable time for the discussion, and *thank* the person for taking the time to talk with you.

   - Make it clear that you're asking for help in solving the problem. Avoid blaming the other person by using "I" language and Tele-visioning.

When you ask, "Why do you want what you want?" you'll discover the underlying issues. For example, you want a window closed, but your co-worker wants the window open. Negotiations will get stuck if you argue about whether the window *should* be open or closed because you'll slide into debates about *truth* or *reasonableness*. Instead, if you ask, "Why do you want what you want?" of yourself and the other person, you may find that one person is cold and the other wants fresh air. Once that's understood, both parties can find a satisfying solution. For instance, the person who wants the fresh air could find a space heater to place by the person who's cold.

The topics we fight about aren't usually the real problem. We argue in marriages about laundry, money, time management, and kids. In our professional lives, we argue about dirty laundry, money, time management, and subordinates. We may complain to our boss, "You need to focus more on team morale," when the truth is that we wanted a promotion. We typically don't stop and figure out what would *fix* the problem before we start an argument. We then fight endlessly about things like who should clean the cat box at home or the lunchroom at work. When you use the **ROAR** technique, you'll ask the right questions, so you'll be able to determine what both of you *really* want. Once you do so, you can attain your goal while still creating a solution that the other person will support.

Toolkit for Connecting in the Heat of Battle

Think of a conflict you're currently having, and let's apply the **ROAR** tool to create cooperation.

1. Have you identified the Real Outcome desired by yourself and the other person? Have you asked, "Why do you want what you want?" What options address both of your concerns? For example, you and your spouse are fighting about how much sex you have. The **Real Outcome** desired by one of you might be to "feel loved," and the **Real Outcome** desired by the other might be to "not feel controlled." If you continue to just fight about having sex 2.5 times a week, you won't talk about options where you can both feel loved and free of control. For instance, the person who wants to "feel loved" might come up with activities other than sex that "feel loving" (like a bath, massage, or intimate conversation). The person who "feels controlled" might be given the power to initiate when and how the couple has sex. When you use the **ROAR** method, you'll only be limited by your creativity in finding solutions.

2. Have you Affirmed the Relationship? What positive thing can you say? For example, with co-workers you don't like, you could say that you value your working relationship or you want to work successfully together. With a difficult friend, you might say you value your history and shared memories. None of the above statements professes undying love, but they leave room for a less-troubled relationship. If you approach someone and say, "You're a jerk, but I have to work with you so we better try to get along," your chances of success are slim.

- Have you set a mutually agreeable time and thanked the person for being open to discussing the issue?

- Are you avoiding blaming by using "I" language and Tele-visioning?

An Example of Connecting in the Heat of Battle

Ned and his business partner, Tamara, were stuck in a tense, long-term argument about whether to grow their business or stabilize it. Ned had told Tamara that she lacked courage and needed to take bigger risks, but she wasn't budging. Ned used the **ROAR** toolkit to find out *why* Tamara wanted to stabilize the business. When Tamara told Ned that they hadn't been able to secure an important business loan yet, he realized that he didn't know about this. Tamara added that she'd be glad to expand the business once they had the loan. When Ned learned to connect with Tamara in the heat of battle, they stopped fighting with each other and started to fight the problems of their business—together.

Four Rituals That Create Cooperation

In addition to using **ROAR**, here are four other habits to develop that will allow you to smoothly navigate any difficult conversation.

#1: State the Outcome You Want

Most of us have good intentions when we enter into a conflict. Then the minute we get mad, we only have one intention—to make the other person wrong. Instead, when you feel the urge to throw a temper tantrum, try using your outcome like a lighthouse in the fog. If you focus on your goals rather than your rage, you'll find that people are more accommodating. If your negotiating partner throws a temper tantrum, you can paraphrase and use "I" language to restate your outcome rather than throwing a fit of your own.

For example, when arguing with a co-worker, you might start by stating, "I'd like to make decisions more as a team." Your co-worker may rant, "There you go again, demanding we do things *your* way. You just want the good projects!" Now you're faced with a decision—do you stick with your goal of teamwork or lower yourself to a conversation about who's the bad guy? If you want to continue discussing collaboration, paraphrase your co-worker and repeat your outcome: "So it sounds like you think I want to do things my way. I actually want to talk to you about doing things together as a team. Can we discuss that?" If you avoid getting hooked into a two-year-old conversation about who's being mean, and keep repeating your outcome, your co-worker has a good chance of supporting *your* goal of teamwork.

Be aware that you don't have to know the solution to the conflict when you make an outcome statement. It's like saying that you want to go to Paris. You don't have to know exactly how to get there. You're simply stating a goal so that you and your partner can move toward it. Then together you can make travel plans. You'll find that people are more interested in *your* goals if part of the solution came from them. The following are examples of outcome statements:

- "I know we disagree about the budget, so I'd like to develop one that we *both* can live with."

- "I'd like to find activities that *both* of us enjoy."

- "I know we disagree about hiring this employee. I want to make sure he can do the job we *both* need."

#2: Ask in Detail How They See the Problem

To improve your understanding of the other person, use questions such as: "What do you think is going on?" "What *specifically* do you want?" "How would [state what they want] be helpful to you?" and "What's your view of this situation?" You can't create a solid solution without seeing the world *in detail* through the eyes of the person you're fighting with.

#3: Paraphrase and Ask for More Information

Your negotiations will fail if you don't have enough information, or if you jump to conclusions. However if you paraphrase in order to find out more, you'll have the data you need to understand the real issues. You'll also give others a chance to vent so that they can settle down and listen to you. You help people feel understood when you ask questions such as: "What is upsetting to you about that?" or "Can you help me understand your viewpoint better?"

The best stance to take during a negotiation is *curiosity*. You can work magic when you use Social Sorcery tools because you'll listen inquisitively, paraphrase, and ask for information rather than engaging in useless, exhausting arguments. Most of us want to jump in and tell other people what a good person we are and how badly they've misinterpreted us—but this won't help! Get rid of the myth that everyone can remain rational during a disagreement. Conflict is an irrational and emotional experience, and people are often inaccurate and negative in their perceptions of us during a quarrel. Your ability to be curious and explore another's viewpoint rather than argue about accuracy or rationality will encourage the other person to eventually listen to *your* ideas.

Keep in mind that if your partner is very emotional, it works best to go back and forth between paraphrasing and asking for more information. People won't listen to your views until they're calmer, so don't get defensive or try to explain your viewpoints.

#4: Ask for What You Want, and Brainstorm Solutions

Restate your **Real Outcome** with the new information you possess, or ask your negotiating partner to help create different options that you both find acceptable. For instance, if you're arguing about where to go on a vacation but find that you both agree on relaxation as the end goal, brainstorm to create a list of relaxing places to visit. You can then discuss *all* the places on the list rather than creating a power struggle where you say, "I insist on Jamaica," and your partner says, "It has to be the Florida Keys."

The Art of Dumb Questions

Most of us have watched at least one episode of *Columbo,* featuring the bumbling and intensely curious detective played by Peter Falk. Week after week, Columbo foiled his criminals by stumbling around in his baggy trench coat and asking a million seemingly stupid questions. In his own way, Columbo demonstrated a basic principle of having the Interpersonal Edge*: Don't be afraid to ask questions—even seemingly stupid ones.* By doing so, you'll eventually figure out what you want to know. The detective also knew a key principle of Social Sorcery: *What you fear or can't tolerate limits your options.* If you can't stand looking or feeling stupid for a few seconds, you often overlook creative possibilities in tough situations. You also miss out on the upside of looking obtuse. When you seem a little "slow," others won't find you intimidating, are more willing to admit *they* don't know, and will reveal information they wouldn't necessarily give to a smoother operator.

When I consult, I feel free to ask seemingly stupid questions. The surprising reality is that many people on the teams I work with don't know the answer, but they *think* they should know, so they fake it. As such, they're usually very relieved when I take the risk to ask something obvious. The moral of this example is that the more you cultivate an attitude of *curiosity* during a conflict, the more likely you are to gather information to create win-win permanent solutions. Looking slightly silly lasts only a second— getting terrific results lasts a lifetime.

When we don't cultivate an attitude of *curiosity,* we're more likely to make genuine fools out of ourselves because it's easier to assume that people are out to get us, and we then take actions based on our false assumptions. Then we really look silly. People usually respond better to others who appear curious about their motives than to folks who automatically assume they have evil intentions.

As you use these tools to deal with conflict, you'll run into a myth that often paralyzes people during a disagreement: Some think that anger is something to avoid during a conflict. In reality, your anger can be an *invaluable* ally that will give you the fuel to set effective limits and motivate others to treat you with respect . . . as you'll discover in the next chapter.

CHAPTER 13

KNOW YOUR BOTTOM LINE

"Anyone can get angry, or give and spend money—these are easy; but doing them in relation to the right person, in the right amount, at the right time, with the right aim in view, and in the right way—that is not something anyone can do, nor is it easy."

— Aristotle

When you have a conflict with other people, anger is a normal emotion. I have a theory that most of us are products of an angry gene pool or our cave-dwelling ancestors wouldn't have survived all the threats they faced. Unfortunately, our modern culture has an emotional caste system, placing people who are highly emotional on a lower rung. To prove we're worthy of membership in the noble, inexpressive crowd, we must anesthetize our rage, ignore it, or get embarrassed if it's obvious we're mad.

Anger as Ally

Our reverence for stoicism shows up in the popularity of movies where the main character faces certain death without batting an eyelash. James Bond is the epitome of this ideal. The entertainment we watch is becoming increasingly violent, and at the same time our society struggles with higher levels of child abuse, domestic violence, murders, and corporate crime. T-shirts like the one that says "No Fear" on the front and on the back, "Really Stupid," are trying to point out that denying emotions may be the problem, not the solution.

Emotions are a physical internal response. When you get angry, you may shake, turn red, or feel your heart pounding. Many of us deprive ourselves of oxygen when we get mad because holding our breath makes it easier to close off our emotions. Unfortunately, not breathing when we're mad also makes it harder to think.

When we believe that other people are going to hurt us, we usually get mad. But our anger is actually coming out of our *belief* about people, not their vicious intent. For instance, as a young child, if you were abandoned (either physically or emotionally) by a parent, you may get furious when someone leaves you. It may feel as if your survival is at stake as you lash out.

Misinterpreting other people's behavior is common. Checking out your interpretation is way more effective, but not natural or common. The goal shouldn't be to avoid anger, but to be able to make *good choices* when you're mad. If you know that you're too upset to be effective, take a time-out and talk to the person later. If you don't take the time to cool off, intense anger will interfere with your ability to remember and utilize any of the tools in this book.

For instance, let's say that you have a good friend who frequently cancels your get-togethers at the last minute. One day she calls and wants to reschedule—again—just before you leave home to meet her. Your heart starts to pound, and what you really want to do is say something cutting and hang up on her, but it occurs to you that this fury probably isn't solely caused by her flakiness, so you tell her you'll call her back. After you get off the phone, you realize that when you were little, your parents didn't keep commitments to you either, and you're still furious about that. You feel deeply hurt and abandoned by your parents' actions and realize that it's because you feel you weren't important.

After you sort out your feelings, you can call your friend back, reveal a little bit about your history, or talk about how important consistency is for you. You can let her know that it's reasonable for her to cancel; however, you need your friends to be reliable. If she continues to cancel, you'll probably make fewer plans with her and become less emotionally available.

It's not unusual for seemingly trivial events to make us feel deeply angry. When the trigger event is small, we often invalidate our feelings. Then we get even madder the next time the same event happens. Your anger is like a finger pointing to an old hurt. When you're really upset, it's never the current-day event *by itself* making you furious. If you give yourself time to explore similar events from your history, you'll notice a pattern in what irritates you. You can then alert people about your trigger areas so they'll be less likely to set you off. When you understand your triggers, you can also be less impulsive, and better able to *consciously* choose effective ways to express your feelings.

Toolkit for Using Anger as an Ally

In order to identify your anger triggers, first think of three events in the last month that made you angry. What theme or pattern do you see here? For instance, did you feel powerless, disrespected, stupid, inadequate, taken for granted, or frightened?

Compare the list from the events that make you mad now with those that made you mad as a kid. Do you notice any similarity? If you can separate out your past from your present, you'll have better control of your anger and your choices in your current relationships.

An Example of Anger as an Ally

Cathy remembered that she got really mad when her brother came over uninvited, when her husband invited guests over for a dinner party without asking her first, and when her friend signed her up to volunteer at her son's school without checking first. In all three situations, she felt angry, dismissed, and invaded.

Cathy recalled that when she was little, she once found out her family was moving when she saw the moving van pull up, her mother would go through her room and her diary repeatedly, and her father chose which college she'd attend. When she used her anger as an ally, Cathy realized that she felt as powerless now as she did when she was dealing with her mom and dad. She realized that she couldn't change what happened in her childhood, but she *could* expect to be respected as an adult. She called her brother and told him to please call before coming over, informed her husband she would help with a party only if he first asked for her assistance, and told her friend that she'd volunteer at school provided that she was consulted first.

Hexes and Consequences

Creating cooperation includes communicating consequences if others don't do what you've requested. If you ask and ask and never offer a consequence for a refusal to comply, few people will do what you've asked. Consider, for example, all the useless nagging parents do with their children.

A friend of mine, Kimberly, was worried that her daughter, Jen, had attention deficit disorder (ADD). I asked Kimberly, "What makes you think Jen has ADD?"

Her frustration rising, she replied, "Jen is constantly doing things that annoy me, no matter what I say."

Since I'm fond of Tele-visioning, I followed up by inquiring, "Can you give me an example of something 'annoying' Jen is doing?"

Kimberly looked thoughtful and said, "Whenever I talk on the phone, Jen is always trying to talk to me."

I then asked my friend, "What consequences do you set when Jen talks to you while you're on the phone?"

"I scold her," Kimberly responded.

I smiled mischievously and asked finally, "Kimberly, if you could be 30 minutes late to work *every* morning, and the *only* consequence you received was a lecture from your boss—would you change your behavior?" Kimberly got the point and started to take away privileges, toys, and fun events when Jen misbehaved. Her daughter suddenly became quite well mannered, and Kimberly stopped worrying that Jen had ADD.

Every day we enter into a life built out of the consequences of our choices. Divorce, promotion, troubled kids, good health, and financial worries are all results of our decisions. When you start using Social Sorcery, you'll notice the power you have to create consequences for yourself and the power you have to apply them to others.

Parenting is one area where we get instant feedback on how well we've set consequences. Children are quick studies about what parents will let them get away with. I remember talking with my client Martin whose son Tad wouldn't get up in the morning. I asked him, "How do you encourage Tad to get up?"

"I yell at him," he replied.

I looked puzzled and inquired, "How would you behave if your manager yelled at you when you played computer games at work?"

Martin said, "I'd get scared and become sneaky." He then realized the consequences of scaring Tad into behaving. He wanted Tad to learn to be responsible not devious.

Many adults are like Martin; we don't think about the power we have in a situation, and we don't want to be considered "mean." When we combine using ineffective consequences with being afraid to make others mad, some of us turn into doormats. Then there are a few folks who act like steamrollers. They may think "tantrums" *are* effective consequences. In the short run, these adults often get what they want. But in the long run, as Abigail Van Buren said, "People who fight fire with fire usually end up with ashes."

Profit or Loss: Let People Choose

Consequences let people know that they'll profit if they co-operate and lose if they don't. You may have noticed that gravity doesn't have a personal grudge toward anyone, *and* it applies to everyone equally. You can argue with gravity all you want—but step out a third-floor window, and wham! You'll experience the unbiased consequences of gravity.

To apply consequences effectively, you want to imitate gravity. To do this you have to be aware of any guilt or fear you have about getting what you want. When you walk into a situation and calmly state what you want, other people have a clear choice to experience the consequence or cooperate. If you walk into a situation agitated and defensive, you'll spend most of your time arguing about who's right.

For instance, when my husband and I built our current house, the subcontractor left globs of grout all over the tile in our downstairs bathroom. The subcontractor tried to convince me that this was the way "the tile looked in Italy," but I've been to Italy and no Italian craftsperson would be caught dead with this slipshod tile job. I could have spent a lot of time arguing about who was right, but instead, I simply agreed with the subcontractor that I was probably being picky. I added that we were in no hurry to close on the house and were going to wait until the tile was done cleanly before we'd sign off on it. The subcontractor tried more arguments, and I agreed with each one. I gave the subcontractor a choice: Redo the tile neatly or wait a long time for payment from the developer. I did this politely, respectfully, and tenaciously. And guess what? The tile was redone.

To apply consequences well, ask yourself what power you have in a difficult situation. Do you have the authority to help someone, exit a relationship, or take away someone's favorite toy? Can you withhold payment, file a complaint, or support a project? In any situation you're in, you *do* have power—the trick is to be aware of the influence you have and use it.

Be forewarned that using consequences is not about acting like a temperamental child. We've all met people who run around expecting perfect treatment and then spouting huffy threats. After a while, these people alienate everyone and lose all credibility. There's a big difference between making threats and setting consequences. Threats are made when we're gripped by strong feelings, angrily state impulsive penalties, and don't *really* plan to follow through. A wife might scream at an unfaithful husband, "That's the last time I put up with your womanizing! I'm calling my lawyer." The husband will ignore the threat if she says this every time she finds out about another woman. If the woman instead says calmly and neutrally, "Here are separation papers. I love you, but I don't trust you anymore," then the husband knows that this is a genuine consequence.

Consequences are related to a particular behavior, are stated calmly, and are always followed through on. If a child throws food on the floor, the food is taken away. If an employee isn't on time, the job is taken away. If a husband cheats, the wife goes away. You'll notice there's a lot of loss when poor decisions are made. It's been jokingly said that "if you play country music in reverse, the dog comes back, the wife comes back, and you get your job back." When poor decisions are made, it's like a country-music song—because things go away. Your job in setting consequences with others is to point out *what* will go away if people make poor choices with you.

When you use the Interpersonal Edge, you're subtle about your negotiations. You don't march in with a list of demands. With a boss who isn't paying you industry standard, you might say, "I like my job and don't want to leave. I want to let you know that recruiters are calling me. I'm not pursuing these offers at this time, but I felt it was only fair to let you know." If the boss wants to keep you, your salary will be raised to at least the industry average. If your boss doesn't take action, you've now learned that your boss won't pay you fairly and a new job may be in order. When you have the Interpersonal Edge, you don't make a threats . . . you make promises. In this example, you would have communicated to your boss that you're valuable and would be going to the highest bidder—which is the consequence of underpaying an employee.

Sometimes you won't notice what you want until a certain issue arises. Let's say you have a new lover and you really like her, but at parties she flirts with all the guys in the room. You can put up with this behavior and become a doormat, or you can be a steamroller, call her unflattering names, and storm out. Or, you could use Social Sorcery and say, "Honey, I've noticed you paying a lot of attention to men at the parties we've been attending. I thought you were my girlfriend. If you pay a lot of attention to the guys at the next party, I'm going to leave because I get really uncomfortable." Notice that you aren't making threats. You aren't speaking in the heat of the moment. You're forewarning her, *and* you'll follow through.

If you know that you aren't prepared to stick to a consequence, don't say it—otherwise you'll teach people to ignore your words. Parents may say, "You're grounded for life," when it's improbable they'll follow through. Better for them to promise, "No social functions for the next week," and mean it.

I remember a conversation with my friend Jim as he was raving about his new love interest. He said glowingly, "It's so great! She has *no* expectations!"

I told him that I thought it unlikely that his new lover had *no* expectations. I said, "In my experience, everyone has expectations. It's just whether they put them on the table in the beginning or not." When we state our expectations up front with others, we get a chance to find out if our needs match. If people would talk first about what they want, many painful endings in professional and personal connections would be avoided. If these discussions don't occur, then both parties develop inaccurate fantasies about what the future holds.

My dear friend Monica learned painfully about the consequences of not exploring expectations. She longed to get married and have a baby, so when she started dating Tom, she told him right away about her goals, but she didn't ask about his. Tom showed her a room in his house during the first month of dating and said, "Wouldn't this make a great baby's room?" Monica quickly decided that this meant Tom wanted to marry *her* and have a baby with *her*.

Six months later, Tom hadn't even said he loved her. When Monica called me, confused and frustrated, I said, "It might have been helpful if you'd asked Tom what he wanted when you two first started to date." I then added, "It's not too late to find out what he wants right now."

So she did. Tom said, "I do want to get married and have kids, but I don't think you and I are a long-term match." And, poof, he was gone. Monica couldn't believe it. Hadn't Tom talked about *their* baby's room? Or had he? If she'd asked him early on about his expectations about their relationship, she would have saved herself from heartbreak.

If you practice and use the tools in this book, you'll move most of your conflicts into cooperation. There will also be times when you use consequences and every other tool of Social Sorcery and still find yourself struggling. In truly difficult relationships, it isn't "cheating" to get help. Most of the folks I truly admire have had superb professional helpers in their life. Corporate mediators, executive coaches, and therapists can save you a painful learning curve. As I stated in the "Impossible People" and "Games Vampires Play" chapters, there are also relationships that can't be fixed. But skilled professionals can even assist with predatory people by helping you identify impossible relationships, advising you on getting out gracefully, and helping you avoid future bad connections.

By learning how to use your anger as an ally and set powerful, appropriate consequences, you'll experience more peace with others in your life. As a result, you'll also have the room to develop an awesome relationship with the one person you can never escape from—yourself. The next chapter will help you connect with your deepest, most powerful, and wisest self.

PART III

IMPROVING EFFECTIVENESS IN THE WORLD

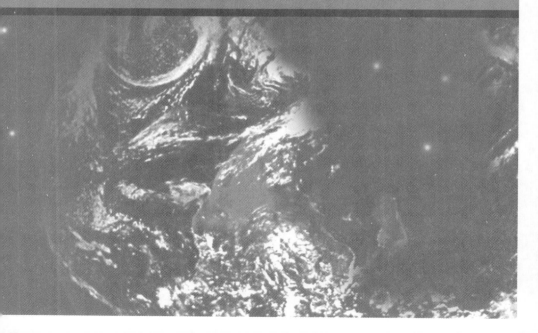

CHAPTER 14

INTUITIVE
MOMENTS

"I want to know God's thoughts, the rest are details."
— Albert Einstein

Some religions maintain that human beings can't access the Divine without the intervention of a representative of that faith. If we all believed that we *required* a religious envoy to connect with or interpret God, then we'd probably give a lot more money and political power to organized religion. But if everybody were able to access the Divine on their own, from within, some religions would lose a lot of their power and profit.

Certain sects (and I won't name names) have insinuated that attempting to directly contact the Divine is not only ineffective but evil. My own experience with my clients is that the deeper they dig into their psyches, the more likely they are to hit the sacred ground of soul. I've found that when people encounter this sacred inner space, they become more intuitive, more compassionate, and wiser.

What Are You Longing For?

As we travel through the world, we sometimes feel homesick but we can't figure out why. It's as if we long for something we can't even remember, but we miss it anyway. Sometimes movies or books capture our imagination because they play with ideas about what we might be longing for. In the movie *Baby Geniuses,* for example, an ambitious, power-hungry CEO, Dr. Kinder, heads BABYCO, the world's largest corporation for baby products. The doctor has a facility full of baby geniuses where she secretly works to crack the code to "baby talk," which she believes is a sophisticated language that allows babies to communicate the secrets of the universe. The babies, however, lose their memory of this language the moment they speak their first actual word.

Sly, age two, is the best and brightest of the baby geniuses, and escapes to the outside world. He then organizes some other babies he meets to invade the lab, free the other baby geniuses, and foil Dr. Kinder's evil empire. The babies, of course, defeat the villains. At the end of the movie, one of the grown-up "good guys" looks deeply into the eyes of one baby and asks if she knows the secrets of the universe. She nods. He takes a deep breath and asks if she will tell him . . . and she says her first word.

The movie is somewhat silly, but it points out our serious longing to know something we dimly remember. We get flashes of memory when we're mesmerized by a beautiful sunset, fall in love, or look into our child's eyes and feel something holy stir. These moments remind us that we're part of something amazing, and hint that we all have a *homing device* pointing us back to our sacred Source.

Perhaps there are things we know that we lose touch with the older we get, but never completely forget. I remember when my daughter was starting to talk, we hadn't taken her to any churches yet, but one day when I asked her, "Where do you think you were before you were born?" she replied simply and patiently (as if I should already know), "In the rainbow, Mama." I asked her what was in the rainbow, and she added, "My buddies." My curiosity piqued, I finally inquired, "Will you see them again?" She sighed, looked like I was trying her patience, and stated, "When I die."

I remember another day when I was telling her that our kitty had been scared of her when she was a baby because she cried so loudly. She walked up to the cat, petted him lovingly, and said matter-of-factly, "Next time I am baby, do not be scared." I asked her what she meant. She explained, "Mama, God makes us all back again." I asked her how she knew that. She said simply, "I just know."

Our longing for "home" and meaning shows up in our search for ultimate knowledge in both science and spirituality. Many people search for clues to the big questions such as "Why are we here?" "What is the meaning of life?" and in my case, "Why does my cell phone go dead on my most important calls?" Sometimes we get excited because we find answers, but sometimes they have an annoying habit of generating bigger questions.

Even though our species passionately pursues "ultimate knowledge," I'm not sure that our bodies are equipped to handle a full experience of our Source. As I was writing this book, I decided to search for a biblical reference at my local library. The librarian who was helping me find Bible passages where people claimed to have experienced God said, "Yup, I remember seeing the movie *The Ten Commandments* and when Charlton Heston [Moses] saw the Burning Bush [the presence of God], he sure came back with a lot of gray hair."

The librarian then found a quote about a time when God and Moses were having a chat. Moses was feeling all warm and fuzzy with God and requested, "Do let me see Your glory!" God responded, "You have found favor with Me and are My intimate friend. My face you can't see, for no man sees Me and still *lives* [italics mine]. Here is a place where you shall station yourself on the rock. When My Glory passes I will set you in the hollow of the rock and will cover you with My hand until I have passed by. Then I will remove My hand, so that you may see My back; but My face is not to be seen."

As my clients work to evolve spiritually, they often express frustration at not being able to fully experience the Divine. I'll point out, "Hey, even historical figures like Moses, who were beloved by God, only got to see a part of Him. Rather than believing that you're unworthy, or that you're not working hard enough, consider that connecting with God *while* in a body is a challenging but worthwhile experience that may have some limits."

Some people claim to have had full contact with the Divine in a near-death experience (NDE). During an NDE, people don't worry about remaining in their bodies since they're "technically dead." Those who've had these experiences often talk about them being moments where a permanent connection with their soul was forged. In some ancient civilizations, it was a common practice to put yourself in life-or-death situations to attain enlightenment. For instance, advanced initiates would enter a pit with poisonous snakes. The theory was that if you were enlightened, you wouldn't be harmed. If you died—well, better luck getting enlightenment next time. Today, most of us would prefer gentler methods with less of a downside.

Introduction to Intuition: Whispers of Wisdom

Laserlike intuition is one of the most valuable tools of a Social Sorcerer. Everything you've learned up until now in this book was designed to give you access to your "sixth sense." Most people have trouble using this sense because hunches come through the body and feelings, which they're not used to interpreting. Because you've been developing more consciousness of your emotions and body, you can now connect more powerfully to your "gut instincts."

When you first try to listen to your hunches, it can be tricky to know the difference between the wise inner voice of Spirit and other destructive internal voices (coming from emotional wounds of the past). Let's say that you want to write poetry. You check with your "gut instincts" and hear the following inner voice: *You can't make money at poetry. Put your energy into something useful.* When an inner voice is critical and negative, you're dealing with your "wounded gut," not your authentic intuition. Our wounded gut is part of the inner predator (covered in Part II), and is fueled by our fear and our desire to avoid pain. Our wounded gut can sound a lot like the negative messages we heard from our family members while growing up.

How do you know if an inner voice is coming from your *wise gut*? I find that it's a good idea to take all inner voices with a grain of salt as you slowly learn to discriminate between positive, negative, or neutral messages. My own experience is that the voice of the soul is gentle, compassionate, patient, and loving toward me and others. Also, I find that this inner voice has a gentle humor about my weaknesses. If an internal voice is abusive, critical, or fearful, I realize that it's not in my best interests to follow that advice.

Through the ages, there has been much spiritual discussion about how to recognize when an inner voice is the voice of the soul. The debate rages hotly when people are trying to access the Divine inside of themselves. Some authors who write about white magic—Dion Fortune, for example—emphasize how important it is for initiates to have some solid counseling before engaging in such tricky inner pursuits. A problem can arise when someone listens to their wounded gut and thinks that they're hearing the voice of God. This type of person can end up committing all sorts of atrocities in the alleged name of religion or Divine guidance.

Since most of us aren't skilled in using our sixth sense, when you first start listening to your intuition you'll notice that the voice of your soul is *whispering,* where the voice of your wounded gut is *shouting.* As you use your wise gut instincts more, however, they'll become louder and clearer.

The following exercise will help you turn up the volume on your intuition and turn *down* the volume on your wounded gut:

Toolkit for Intuition

1. Get a small notebook and carry it around with you. Whenever you notice a thought "whispering" in your head, write it down. You might find yourself frequently thinking about a friend you haven't seen for a while, you may keep having the feeling that you need to make a call about a job you want, or perhaps you'll even get the notion that you should have your brakes checked.

Write down as many of your subtle thoughts as you can. At the end of the week, go through your list and ask yourself which ones feel fearful and which feel loving. Use a highlighter to select the loving ones, and pay particular attention to the thoughts that repeat themselves.

2. Take action on some of the thoughts that continue to come to mind. Note: This isn't permission to behave in any illegal, immoral, or hurtful way, so use good judgment. If you've been thinking about making a particular phone call, do so and see what happens. If you have a repetitive, fearful thought, don't necessarily ignore it. If you keep worrying about a possible disease, it could be the voice of your intuition or fear. You'll only learn to discriminate between these voices over time. Since it doesn't hurt to get checked out, see your doctor. Anytime you're anxious, if there's information you can gather, then do so.

3. Notice your subtle perceptions of others. Do you trust them? Do you think they're secretly sad, or feel that they're hiding something? Act as if a wise advisor had given you this information and check out your impressions. If you think that people are sad, ask how they're feeling. If you think that they're hiding something, ask if there's anything they forgot to tell you. Sometimes your wounded gut will tell you things that are lies, such as "Nobody is safe." Again, if you check out your impressions, you'll learn how to distinguish between your wise and wounded gut.

An Example of Intuition

Deidre had suddenly started to worry about her brakes even though she'd just had them replaced. She was planning a journey over a mountain pass with her family and kept having a feeling of dread about the trip. She felt silly, but decided to take her car back to her mechanic two days before her trip. And it was a good thing she did, because he found that a brake line had been incorrectly tightened. Under city driving conditions, the car might have been fine, but if Deidre had taken the car over the pass, her chances of having a serious accident would have been great. Her intuition may have saved her family's life.

As you get used to listening to your intuition, you'll notice an invisible track laid out for you by your soul each day. This is the optimally effective way for you to go through your day. If you use your wise gut, mundane activities will become touched by the sacred. You'll have an uncanny sense of timing about everyday activities, such as when to call a friend, when to go shopping, or when to take a walk.

For example, when my husband and I built our house several years ago, we were overwhelmed with our lack of knowledge about the process. One day my intuition was loudly whispering to go check out an open house by a certain builder. I hadn't planned on going anywhere that day but had the strong sense that someone I needed to meet was there. We went to the open house, and on our way to the front door, a lovely couple was leaving the home. We started talking to them, and they turned out to be our guardian angels. They'd recently gone through the home-building process and were extremely helpful and generous in their advice and mentoring.

Introduction to Dreams: Soul Letters

Sigmund Freud, the father of psychoanalysis, called interpretation of dreams "the royal road to a knowledge of the unconscious activities of the mind." Well, I believe that dreams are the royal road to your soul, not just your unconscious mind. As you get connected to your intuition, you'll be amazed to find the wise counsel, prophetic advice, and spiritual guidance available to you every night. You don't need to be a dream expert to benefit from your nightly theater, though, and neither do you have to understand every dream symbol. In this section, I'll give you some basics about dreams and teach you how to remember them.

Swiss psychologist Carl Jung, a colleague of Freud's, described dreams as the unopened letters of the soul. Some religions even call sleep "the little death." Most of us know that something happens inside our heads every night, but our memories are usually hazy or nonexistent. If our soul *does* communicate this way, then most of us aren't getting this precious information because we typically don't remember our nightly visions.

When I talk to people about dreams, they often declare that they never have any. Now the truth is that everybody dreams every night. When psychologists do experiments to induce psychosis, one technique is to deprive people of the dream stage of sleep. Thus, as I explain to my clients, if you aren't psychotic, it means that you're having dreams but just don't remember them. If you want a quick litmus test for the strength of your connection with your inner life (or someone else's), ask how often dreams are recollected. The stronger your connection with your inner emotional world, the more often and completely you'll remember your dreams.

It's not necessary to recall *all* your dreams. At one point in my own therapy, I was remembering eight or ten a night. Although the epic stories unfolding in my psychic landscape were fascinating and informative, I'm now content to remember one or two every night. When I'm busy with my outer world, my dreams may even retreat so quickly in the morning that I only remember fragments. The main benefit of opening up this channel is that your intuition has a way of getting messages to you via your nocturnal movies.

Recalling your dreams doesn't happen automatically. If you want to increase your dream memory, you can use the following technique:

> Put a pad of paper or a small recorder by your bed. As you drift into sleep, you're in what hypnotists call a "highly suggestible state." Repeat over and over in your mind: "I will remember my dreams." When you wake up, write

down or tape any fragment you recall. It's essential that you write any image or impression immediately. Don't get frustrated because you may have to try for a couple of weeks before you have dream memories. Be patient and think of remembering dreams like fishing: You may have your hook in the water awhile before you get a tug. If you give up, you'll never catch the fish swimming through your dreaming mind.

When you have a dream and want to know what it means, skip the books that promise to interpret every dream image. Instead, just write down the symbols, people, or things in your dream. Then write down some words you associate with that person, symbol, or thing. You'll now have a more accurate dream interpretation than most books will provide.

There are a few symbols in dreams that tend to have similar meanings for nearly everyone. For instance, water is a common symbol, and it's associated with emotion. If you dream of a pond, you *may* be dreaming about a small emotion. If you dream about the ocean, you *may* be dreaming about strong emotion or the unconscious. The trick in dream interpretation is to emphasis *your* associations to a symbol, however, not the *usual* meaning.

My clients who've gone through intensive therapy tell me that they have dreams about being able to breathe under water as they explore the deepest oceans. These clients are at home in a world of deep and wild emotions. At the start of therapy, one client, Margaret, dreamed that she was in a wading pool that gradually became deeper and turned into the ocean. As she swam out to the deeper end of the pool, she could see the sea, so she got scared and went back to the wading pool. Margaret's dream was telling her that she needed to take her therapy slowly, and it gave her a preview of the deep and mysterious emotional waters ahead.

There are three levels of dream interpretation. In the first, assume that everything in the dream is a symbol for a part of you—your boss, any animals, the setting—everything. The person in the dream that looks like the current you is the part you know consciously.

You may have a dream where your current self goes into a dark cave. Once inside, you see dangerous animals and beautiful jewels, and you may have to get through the animals to get to the jewels. This dream could be telling you that there are primitive parts of you living in the dark that guard precious inner resources. To find these "jewels," you'll need to venture into the unknown and deal with aspects of yourself that seem threatening. The jewels, animals, and cave are all aspects of your inner psyche. The current you in the dream is your conscious ego. It's as if your psychic landscape stages a play each night tailored for your specific education. All the actors and the setting of the dream are carefully chosen to communicate information to help you.

Sometimes you may not see yourself in a dream but are witnessing others. For instance, I have a very cautious client, Kendra, who recently dreamed that she was watching a male friend of hers slowly climb down a cliff. She sees herself as a person who doesn't take risks even though she's making many brave changes right now. When I asked Kendra about her associations to the guy in the dream, she said, "He's someone I haven't seen in a while." I chuckled and observed, "So the part of you that takes risks is a part that you haven't been aware of in a while." You'll notice that dream interpretations aren't usually literal. The dream wasn't telling Kendra that she was about to take up cliff climbing.

Assuming that everything in the dream is about you is difficult when the dream includes a malevolent, frightening, or uncomfortable person or situation. Many years ago I dreamed that I was in a building being chased by a crazy, homicidal woman. When I woke up, I wasn't thrilled to consider this off-putting part of me, but the dream wasn't saying that I was in danger of becoming a serial murderer. Instead, it was highlighting a self-destructive area of my psyche.

Another common uncomfortable dream is that you're having sex with someone of the same gender or a friend's spouse. These dreams can worry people but don't indicate that you're switching sexual orientations or planning to break a friend's heart. Sex in dreams is about longing for a union that has the qualities you desire. Of course you may also be learning about your sexuality, but you don't need to take your dreams *literally* without considering the symbolic meaning first.

The second level of dream interpretation is to look at what the dream is telling you about relationships in your life. If you dream that your husband is cheating on you, it doesn't hurt to tell him the dream so that he can think about its meaning. Sometimes you may be getting an early warning that he's interested in someone else, or the two of you are growing distant. The dream may also only be about yourself (which would be the first dream level).

When I was newly married, I dreamed that my husband went on a date with a woman named Ophelia. When I woke up, I poked him and said accusingly, "*You* were on a date with Ophelia." He rubbed his sleepy eyes, looked at me adoringly, and chuckled. I could then see that the dream was about me, as it was referring to a part of me that doesn't feel safe with people. Since that dream, Ophelia has become a joke between us. At one point when I was using my husband's cell phone, I found a listing for Ophelia. I asked my husband about the number, and he told me to dial it. I did, and it was the number for my own work phone!

At other times, a dream can be telling you about real issues in your relationships. You may dream that your boss is undermining you, your mother is ill, or your co-worker is pregnant. These dreams, again, are not *necessarily* literal. Pregnancy can indicate a new possibility, illness could mean being emotionally or physically unwell, and being undermined might refer to many things.

The third level is what some native cultures call the "Big Dream." It is dreamed by an individual *within* a tribe but is meant for the *entire* group. In some tribal cultures, these Big Dreams provide guidance for decisions affecting the whole community. In these dreams, you may see yourself observing a scene, or you may hear a voice come from the sky. Big Dreams have a feeling of numinousness or the sacred, and they're hard to forget.

I've had several Big Dreams, and three of them stand out. I had the first one in my early 20s when I started in-depth therapy, and I was feeling like a wimp because I was so emotional all the time. In the dream, I was in an audience, in front of a Buddha-like old man. I'd started to cry and couldn't stop. I was brought in front of the man and felt terribly embarrassed. As I stood there sobbing, he looked at me with great tenderness, kindness, and respect, saying, "Very, very good! Here is one with the strength to feel!" When I woke up, it was the first time it had occurred to me that feeling deep emotion takes strength. This dream has been invaluable to me in honoring and appreciating the emotional courage required for myself and my clients to experience strong emotion. I've often told my clients this dream when they're coming alive emotionally and feeling self-conscious.

I had the second dream on the night of my 29th birthday. Astrologers and human-development experts believe that the transition from 29 to 30 is the beginning of *real* adulthood. I dreamed that I was standing in front of a tunnel of white light that was swirling around in a circular fashion. My mother was standing between the tunnel and me. In the tunnel were indistinct beings who I knew loved me and were waiting for me. I knew that once I stepped into the tunnel, I'd be dead. As I witnessed the scene, I heard a voice say with loud authority, "The only thing really important to do in life is to create your dream!" I knew when I woke up that between here and death, it was important to remember that we're *all* here to create our dreams. Shortly after this dream, I started my business.

In the third Big Dream, I was watching Jesus and the devil engage each other. The devil was very seductively trying to get Jesus to agree to be absorbed into him. As I was observing the scene, Jesus agreed, and the devil started to absorb Jesus into himself. I was ineffectively shouting, "No, don't do it, bad idea!"

As I watched Jesus be absorbed into the devil, I *knew* that the devil started to feel this indescribable level of love within his body, and as he felt this love, all the numbness in him started to soften. As his deadness thawed and the devil started to feel, I watched him collapse into himself, sobbing with pain. As I watched in amazement, I realized that what appears "evil" in myself and in others is actually just devoid of love, and thus, devoid of feeling. I also could see that all those spiritual texts saying that "love is the answer" are *literally* correct. As I awoke, I was keenly aware of the raw power behind the kind of love I'd witnessed in the dream. If we, as a species, could learn to harness this energy, most of the world's problems could be solved.

In working with my clients (and myself), I've noticed how our soul appears to be clever in its ability to weave humor and our life history into our dreams. There's nothing in any of our dreams that's accidental. I've heard it said that dreams have the job of a heavily censored newspaper in a dictatorship, the latter being our conscious perception of ourselves. Our dreams try to tell us the things we ignore, avoid, or don't want to know—and we thought our jobs were tough!

Let's try an exercise to understand dream messages.

Toolkit for Dreams

Write down a dream or dream fragment you recently had: (**Example:** *I dreamed I tried to dial 911 and couldn't get through.*)

Now write down any memories, associations, or feelings you had in this dream: (**Example:** *I felt scared; it reminded me of trying to get Mom to help me; I felt powerless.*)

Now think about any situations in your life where you've felt this way.

What information might your dream be providing that you can use while you're awake?

An Example of Dreams

Carrie repeatedly dreamed that she had a baby and kept forgetting to feed it, but the baby didn't die. In her dream, she felt panicky, guilty, and distracted. In her waking life, Carrie had just started a new creative business and had also just found out that her husband had prostate cancer. She was very worried that she was too distracted for her new business to survive. As she used the dream toolkit, she realized that her new business was the baby, and that it would survive even if she didn't "feed" it right now. She relaxed, took care of her husband, and it turned out that both he and her business came through that difficult time just fine.

If you keep notes about your dreams, you'll become more curious about deciphering the symbols of "dream speak." One way that you can translate your dream images is to keep a journal by your bed so that you see your dream themes change over time. If you have a powerful dream or nightmare, put yourself in a position where you're sitting comfortably (with your head unsupported or you'll go to sleep). Visualize or imagine that you're reentering the dream, and talk to the characters or things in it (a river, butterfly, or bridge can all talk back and give you information).

If you find it hard to visualize, then try this exercise on paper: Write the name of a dream character or thing down and then imagine what it says. Then write *your* name down and respond back and forth until there's a dialogue between you and the dream symbol.

The next chapter will help you develop your intuition and gut instincts even further by anchoring your soul into your body with yoga, meditation, and the ability to learn spiritual lessons from your everyday experiences.

🌍 🌍 🌍

CHAPTER 15

INVESTING IN BLISS

*"The new frontier lies not beyond the
planets but within each one of us."*
— Pierre Elliot Trudeau

Some folks believe that people who have great intuition or
a good spiritual connection are simply lucky. They then decide
they're powerless to develop such "good fortune." In reality, I find
that many people who enjoy the benefits of accurate hunches and
divine guidance commonly use three practices: yoga, meditation,
and developing a relationship with an "inner guru." You can invest
in any or all three of these disciplines to expand your peace of mind.
It's easier to use your Interpersonal Edge tools when you know how
to be in the eye of the hurricane during the storms of life.

Yoga: The Enchantment of the Body

*Y*oga comes from an ancient language, Sanskrit, and means "union" or "yoking." There are parts of yoga that seem to relate solely to physical exercises; however, these are actually ancient postures that help us fully incarnate our souls into our bodies. There are esoteric texts that argue about *when* a soul fully incarnates during the birth process, but if you practice yoga, you'll be amazed to discover how much of your awareness is still hanging outside your body. You'll discover emotions, muscles, and sensations that will surprise you, and you'll learn that your body is an amazing universe you haven't fully explored.

Complete consciousness of your body is darn near impossible, but the effort to be fully conscious makes for interesting discoveries. Underlying all forms of yoga is the belief that human beings are more than the physical body. Hinduism speaks of our true identity being a nonphysical Self (also known as *atman* or *purusha*), which is eternal and inherently blissful.

The actual practice of yoga can feel anything but blissful. The physical exercises may lead you to painful, numb, or disconnected places in your body. The interesting thing about these postures, though, is that you're *choosing* to find these uncomfortable places. In life, it's more common for us to wait until pain seeks us out. When, instead, you *choose* to find the pain, breathe into it, and experience it—well, that's volunteering for enlightenment.

As you find your tight, painful, or numb areas, you'll enhance your physical well-being, but that's not the biggest reward. The most wonderful result is increasing your awareness, your connection with your soul, and your sense of purpose. Imagine that every human being is an electrical circuit of aliveness. As you use the tools of Social Sorcery, you'll be running larger and higher volts of electricity through your body, and yoga will increase your ability to accept greater degrees of this current. As you step up your capacity for feeling and aliveness, you'll bring more of your whole self into your physical form.

As you perform the postures, you may also experience many of the same emotions that you do when you encounter interpersonal challenges. When you can't do a posture, you may feel embarrassed, get mad, or be demoralized. Any posture in yoga is a great metaphor for how we react to challenges in life. Do we feel ashamed when we can't do something perfectly? Are we so busy wishing that we could do it differently that we hold our breath and get mad at ourselves? Can we acknowledge where we'd like to be and still accept where we are and relax?

I remember a yoga class where we were all struggling with a difficult posture. Doing the full posture would mean that we could bend over from a standing position and put both hands flat on the floor. No one in the class could do it, and we were all obviously frustrated. My teacher looked at us, sighed, and gently said, "You know, I've been to the floor—there's nothing there." We then chuckled and remembered that it was the journey, not the destination, that would help us.

It's easier to have the Interpersonal Edge when you honor and care for your body. The consciousness you're developing will be helped along when you have a healthy physical vehicle. In our culture, we're fairly obsessed with the pursuit of physical beauty through diet and exercise, but that's not the goal of yoga. Although you *will* get physically stronger, the challenge is to integrate your insides with your outsides.

If you want to learn how to do yoga, use your intuition to look for a teacher who feels right to you. Although there are many videos and books available, learning the discipline from another person is usually more successful. When you evaluate instructors, pay attention to the different energies they bring to the class. A highly effective teacher is humble, patient, loving but challenging, and sincerely walking on a spiritual path. A helpful leader cares more about the process of learning than the end goal, and more about the student than the teacher being right. You'll also find that certain yoga teachers will share philosophies and lifestyle ideas that will be helpful in nurturing your soul.

If you learn yoga, another tool for developing your intuition—meditation—will be easier. As you physically strengthen and stretch your body during the practice, habitual aches and pains will fade. You'll become more relaxed physically, be more at ease when you sit, and be able to experience deeper meditation.

Meditation: Entering the Sanctuary

If prayer is when you talk to God, then meditation is when you listen. It's been said that thoughts in our minds are like monkeys in trees, because our thoughts jump from one distracting idea to the next. In meditation, you let go of your thoughts so that you can enter the sanctuary within. Although the final goal is noble, beginning meditators mostly feel agitated, bored, or upset—pretty much anything but spiritual. Good meditation teachers will tell you that this is normal and that it takes practice to quiet down. In fact, it can take three months or longer before a beginning meditator really grasps the benefits of being still.

As your body gets used to meditating, you'll develop more of a relaxation response, and learn how to enter your internal sanctuary. At this point, meditation is physically rewarding. It can feel like you're floating on a warm tropical wave in the ocean as the stress flows out of your body. Each meditation technique has a slightly different foundation, but they all have the same basic goal. The Buddhists may say you enter the Buddha, the Christians may say you have a personal relationship with Christ, and the Transcendental Meditation folks may say you become one with the unified field. There are many types of meditation practices out there, and experimenting to find one you can stick with is important.

When you practice meditation consistently, your ability to stay in the "eye of a hurricane" during life's storms will increase. You'll also find that meditating strengthens your inner connections. Emotions you didn't previously notice, your intuitive voice, and solutions to problems you're having will all be easier to hear in the silence of your internal haven.

Meditation is the 24-hour, open-to-all-spiritual-beliefs temple located conveniently wherever we are. When you meditate, you're reminded on a daily basis that there's a place inside of you where you're never alone (surrounded by Divine affection), a place inside you where you're always safe (no matter what else is going on), and a place inside you that is unchanging.

A few years ago, I accompanied a relative to a cemetery on a beautiful spring day, where there were many people wandering about. I was walking around reading the inscriptions on the gravestones and was keenly aware of being surrounded by so much loss. At the same time, the sun was shining and everything was in bloom. As I looked around me, I thought about what a paradox it is to live in a world where a good life means that you love people and then they die on you. In a world where change is the only constant, meditation reminds us of what is eternal.

Toolkit for Meditation

Here are the basics of meditation:

Set aside at least 20 minutes, and find a quiet place where you won't be disturbed. Then choose a meaningful word. It can be *love,* a spiritual teacher's name, or *om* (which is said to be the sound of the universe). You can also focus on your breathing. Then sit comfortably with your head unsupported. As you close your eyes, say your word internally, or focus on your breath. Notice your thoughts, but keep returning to your word or your breath. Your thoughts will distract you before you know it. Don't worry, you're still meditating correctly—just return to your word and breath. If you feel any physical discomfort, resettle your body. If you're feeling any emotion, notice it. Meditation develops the ability to witness what you're thinking or feeling without judging it. If you're very tired, your head will bob or fall forward into a light sleep. Meditation puts you in touch with what your body needs, whether that is rest, food, or emotional release.

Meditation programs make different recommendations about when you meditate and how often. In general, good times are right after you wake up and during the late afternoon. You can start by trying it once a day and gradually add another session. I'd recommend not meditating on a full stomach because your body will have trouble trying to digest food and rest at the same time.

Becoming One with a <u>Very</u> Dusty World

I remember spending every spare minute of my first two years of college looking for a book that would reveal the mysteries of the universe. I figured that somebody must have found the secrets already and if they had . . . well they must have written them down. I read books on ancient mythology, magic, human nature, and texts on virtually every religion. One day as I sat amidst the musty library shelves on a rainy day doggedly pursuing the Truth, a persistent and disturbing thought occurred to me: If someone *had* found the Truth and had written it down, even if I discovered the text it wouldn't do me any good because I probably wouldn't understand it. I realized right then, at age 19, that I'd have to go out, live my life, and experience a lot more before I would be able to comprehend certain facets of universal wisdom.

The tools I'm offering you in this chapter will open the window to your soul to a greater extent. As you connect more deeply to your innermost self, you may find it difficult to talk about your new experiences. Lao-tzu, a Chinese philosopher, said in the 6th century B.C.: "He who knows does not speak. He who speaks does not know. Close the mouth. Shut the door of desire. Blunt the sharpness. Untie the tangles. Soften the light. Become one with the dusty world." Many spiritual texts echo Lao-tzu's idea that it's challenging to find the right words to talk about our most profound spiritual knowledge. I think there are two reasons why:

1. It's almost impossible to find the exact words to adequately describe the experience.

2. Even if somebody could tell you, it wouldn't make sense if you aren't ready to hear it.

The Zen Buddhists gave up on even trying to talk about "it" and developed Zen koans. These are questions designed to encourage the student to "think outside the box." A classic koan is: "What is the sound of one hand clapping?" Students have to expand their definition of sound because the answer is "silence."

I have found that our culture encourages us to trust the expertise of *external* authorities much more than our society encourages us to develop our own *inner* authority. Many of my clients come to me believing that I know more than they do about what they need to do. I tell them, "If you learn to trust me more than yourself, I will just be one more person who disconnected you from your most powerful teacher—your own soul. My job is to listen to you deeply enough so that I can then help you listen to *yourself* and teach you how to connect with your *own* authority."

In sum, you don't have to spend your life looking for a powerful external guru. You'll find that this wise soul is already inside of you waiting for you to listen to her or him. As you use Social Sorcery, the wise voice of your internal guru will become clear, strong, and easily accessible to you.

I encourage you to learn from your inner guru to find your own answers. Joseph Campbell, author and expert on mythology, was fond of saying that he didn't believe in God; he believed in his own experience, and he *had* an experience of God. The best teachers I've encountered may not have been able to tell me *everything*, but they did a great job of putting me in a position to be coached by my inner wisdom.

As you become one with the very dusty world, you'll start to notice an intelligent pattern unfolding in your life. Events, people, and even problems will seem less random. You'll expand your relationship skills beyond yourself, beyond other people, and into the world around you. Your life will become a conversation between you and an intelligent, alive universe.

The next chapter introduces you to the classroom you're already in—your Life Lab.

CHAPTER 16

COSMIC MOMENTS

*"Have patience with everything unresolved in your heart
and to try to love the questions themselves as if they were
locked rooms or books written in a very foreign language.
Don't search for the answers. . . . Live the questions now."*

— Rainer Maria Rilke

With the Interpersonal Edge, your relationship issues will look less random and more like a pattern. As you implement your new communication tools, you'll realize that curiosity is more helpful than certainty—especially when dealing with the frustrating aspects of life. When you apply Social Sorcery, you'll become more aware that you're a scientist in what I call the Life Lab. This lab gives you feedback about your behavior through the results you obtain. If you don't like your results, you need to learn more about the laws governing your experiments and change your approach. The Life Lab is particularly fond of using relationships with other people as a teaching tool.

The Universal "Help" Menu

Just as there is in a computer program, there's a "Help" menu available in the Life Lab—if you know where to look. The challenge is that this menu is written in the spiritual language of symbols. The language of *Spirit* is, for most of us, "like books written in a foreign tongue," because it uses relationships, metaphors, and dreams to communicate. For you to access the Help menu of the language of Spirit, you need to be able to translate the words.

You can start learning this language by imagining that an invisible spiritual author is writing "the script" of your life. Presume that this author is trying to wake you up from who you think you should be and remind you of who you really are. You can even dare to dream that the invisible author is reminding you that within you lies a "sleeping magician" who knows how to bring all of your dreams to life. Contemplate the fact that the word *imagine* contains the letters "I" and "mage," and that *mage* means "magician." When we *i-mag-ine*, we use the magic of our creativity to visualize the life we want. You can finish this exercise by considering the possibility that every event, situation, conflict, seemingly accidental occurrence, and dream is uniquely composed for you by an unseen spiritual genius who plans to educate, empower, and rouse the real you.

The chapter on dreams taught you that the first level of dreamwork uses every person, event, and object as part of your personality. What if you approached every day as a "waking dream," where everything and everyone was part of your greater self? When I teach workshops on dreams, I give my students an exercise to do at lunch. I ask them to go somewhere and write what they observe for ten minutes. When my students return, we pretend that what they saw was a "waking dream" full of meaning for each individual.

For instance, my student Tina went to the park one day and saw a loving mother and her baby playing. There were many other dramas unfolding at the park, but this particular scene captured Tina's imagination. When she worked with the "waking dream" in class, she realized that her relationship with her own mother had recently improved. She also saw she'd become kinder and gentler with herself due to the "inner work" she'd done. Tina could see that her fascination with the baby and mother reflected her own internal changes.

When I ask students to try this exercise, I find that even if they go to the same place, their stories are still unique. Either life is just one big projection screen reflecting us back to ourselves, or the universe is well orchestrated by invisible hands to help us learn (and maybe both suppositions are true).

If you imagine that everything is communicating to you all the time, you'll probably look at your world through different eyes. Just like interpreting your nightly dreams, some messages might jump out at you, some might be subtle, and some might be difficult to understand. Even if the events of your life are random, you'll find that you can make a meaningful pattern out of the chaos. This will allow you to benefit from everything that happens to you.

What I know for certain is that the more I learn, the less I know for certain. I lost interest in cornering the market on the "Truth" a long time ago. Nowadays I'm more interested in using my most effective recent theory and keeping my mind open to improve on it when new data becomes available.

☽ O ☾

Messages that come to us in the form of experiences can appear mundane. We may end up missing them if we aren't paying attention. For example, in my last year of high school, I lost my keys. Since I'm usually well organized, their disappearance was a real puzzle. During the few days that the keys were lost, I was also giving intense thought to what I wanted to do in my life. After a week of searching, I picked up my high school psychology text and found the keys beneath it. I froze, looked at the keys, looked at the psychology text, and knew that the key to fulfillment in my professional life would be found in psychological work.

Until that moment, there was nothing about the loss of the keys that had seemed like anything but an annoying memory lapse, but what makes events more than mundane annoyances is the timing, the symbolism, and your awareness of connections between yourself and the event.

For instance, my client Rose left a session one day thinking about quitting therapy. Although she was making big changes, she was also very scared. As Rose drove away from my office, she immediately got stuck behind a commercial truck with writing on the back door that said: "Fix It, Don't Forget It." As soon as she turned the corner, she ended up behind a business van that said: "Do It Now, Why Wait?" Similar things happened throughout the week. At her next session, Rose told me that she swore the universe was conspiring to keep her in therapy.

The universe can also speak to you in less-obvious metaphors using physical objects in your world. In my childhood home, the kitchen knives were rusty and dull, but although my parents would complain about them, they never got around to sharpening them. If I use the "waking dream" exercise on the rusty knives in my childhood kitchen, I associate aggression and boundaries with them. In addition, they were in the kitchen, which is a metaphor to me for nurturing. The "waking dream" exercise would help me see that my family's difficulty with expressing anger and setting limits made nurturing each other difficult. Not surprisingly, in my personal therapy, I worked extensively on aggression and boundaries (sharpening my knives). My ability to recognize when I'm getting mad and set limits with others has made profound differences in my marriage, my parenting, and my life as a whole.

The universe is patient, and it has a great sense of humor. If you stay alert, you'll see that you're getting the same lesson through body symptoms, coincidences, or conflicts in increasingly obvious ways—until you get it. For instance, my client Melissa had a boss who was verbally abusive, but she was afraid to confront him. First she began having trouble with her eyesight. Then, after her boss chewed her out one day, her car radiator blew up. Next she started getting prank phone calls, where someone was yelling at her. When Melissa broke out in a rash around her throat, she decided that she'd had enough. She talked to her boss the next morning and told him she couldn't work productively if his behavior continued, and he actually decided he'd rather change than lose her.

After the conversation, Melissa caught a glimpse of her face in a mirror and noticed that her eyes were sparkling and her lips were bright red (from telling the truth, not lipstick). Even if her boss hadn't responded well, she would have felt freed from her fear of confrontation.

I find Divine help everywhere, from billboards to messages in fortune cookies. Sometimes I even ask the universe questions, knowing that events will arise in my life to guide me. The other day while driving, I was internally arguing with myself about whether I should take some new risks with my career. On the one hand, I felt that the universe was giving me encouragement to try new things; on the other, it's sometimes tough for me to trust it. In the middle of my internal debate, I pulled up behind another car at a red light. A large bumper sticker on the car said simply: "God is good." I chuckled, felt supported, and was able to quit worrying so much.

In the Life Lab, you either get to volunteer for enlightenment or you get dragged, kicking and screaming—not being on the path isn't an option. If you keep hitting the enlightenment snooze button, the issues you're avoiding will creatively hunt you down and make you miserable. If you volunteer to deal with your issues, you'll avoid the pain of unnecessary suffering and get more control over your life.

I realize that translating bumper stickers, kitchen utensils, and fortune-cookie messages might seem a little abstract right now, so let's start expanding your ability to speak Spirit by checking out the easiest source of information—your relationships. The beauty of other people is that we love them and hate them but can't live without them. Thus, we're provided with useful data every day in the form of attractions and repulsions. (But you can still play around with those fortune-cookie messages!)

Changing Patterns Through Relationships

Social Sorcerers use relationship difficulties to help them become wiser. I remember one week when several people felt that I'd intentionally harmed them. An association president was angry because I was unavailable to speak to her group, a woman yelled at me because she thought I had cut in line, and a friend was angry because I couldn't help her move. As I thought about these three events, I could see how I immediately apologized and took responsibility for the situation so these people would stop being mad. In each case, I hadn't *intended* harm, but ended up feeling as if the situation were my fault anyway. I could also see how anxious I became when people got mad at me.

When I saw my theme, I used my toolkits to change my behavior. I became aware of how often my parents blamed me when they were upset. I could see that taking responsibility and apologizing calmed my parents down and kept me safe when I was little. I realized that I was no longer a small, helpless child who had to soothe large, scary people. I paraphrased people's anger rather than avoiding it, and used "I" language to state my perceptions. If the other person escalated into rage, I set a limit and stopped the conversation. In one way, this was a tough week; in another, it was rich in liberating options.

My friends sometimes humorously answer my question, "How have you been lately?" with "I've had a lot of learning opportunities," which is a Social Sorcery translation for "It's been tough!" When you have the Interpersonal Edge, you'll develop a sense of humor that will help you cope when you hit rough spots in life. In addition, the toolkits will help you turn the lemons of any tough circumstance into lemonade by showing you how your soul is using these events to help you grow more powerful.

Toolkit for Changing Patterns Through Relationships

Recall the last four times you were upset with a relationship and what upset you. Describe each situation on a separate piece of paper.

How are these situations similar? For example, did you feel powerless, disrespected, or invalidated?

We're all in a classroom, even after we leave formal schooling. The classroom, however, is often involuntary education. If you can *see* the patterns behind what's painful for you, you'll know what courses you're currently studying. Perhaps you're in "Getting Over Being a Doormat 101" or "Predator Animals Don't Make Good Playmates 203" or "Figuring Out What You Came Here to Do 405." You have to see your pattern before you can cooperate with your spiritual curriculum.

An Example of Changing Patterns Through Relationships

Madeleine was upset with her last four bosses. She thought that each one had passed her over for promotions, given her mindless tasks, and failed to see her talents. When she used this toolkit, she also saw that with each boss she worked hard then waited silently for rewards and acknowledgment. Madeleine realized that she'd been in a classroom called "Speak Up or Get Ignored," and she became more vocal about the high-visibility projects she wanted to work on. She was surprised to find that her boss not only gave her most of what she requested, but he also tapped her for *his* position when he was promoted. When she asked why he gave her his job, he said, "Because you know what you want, ask for it, and work hard to earn it."

Using difficulties in life and relationships as a way to get to know your soul isn't something that's commonly done in our culture. We live in a world that mostly assumes relationships ought to make us feel good, secure, and comfortable.

Dr. Franklin, a professor in one of my undergraduate psychology classes, used to tease the students about our collective interest in avoiding pain. Dr. Franklin would jokingly point out how difficult it is to learn from our mistakes if we're being "comfort junkies." He'd say, "Ignorance is bliss! If you pay attention . . . you might see lots of problems. Fixing problems means you have to do things that are a drag. Take my advice, try to be purposely ignorant and you'll never be *uncomfortable*." When a student was avoiding change and bringing the same life problem repeatedly to class, Dr. Franklin would give the class a wicked smile and joke, "Ah . . . another moment of bliss!" Then he'd mischievously chuckle and say with mock seriousness to the student, "Now whatever you do next—don't learn *anything* from this."

Feeling Good All the Time?

Most love songs communicate the message that relationships should make us feel good. Many of these songs proclaim that somewhere, someplace, there's a person who will fix our life, make us feel good all the time, and rescue us from the normal pain of life. If we believe the songs and try to find such a "soul mate," we'll end up searching for a god rather than a human partner.

Some love songs describe how we suffer when our expectations aren't met, but we can still hope for "some enchanted evening" in the future. Both the songs of disappointment and the songs of hope tell us to look for our soul in another person's eyes.

I've made up some typical love song lyrics to point out the myths we hold about relationships: "Dream lover you are my destiny / I can't live without you / Love is all I need / We will never hurt each other / I know you'll never let me down / You're my soul mate because you make me feel good / You are perfectly perfect / You are an angel / As long as you love me, it doesn't matter what you've done."

The last lyric is catchy but frightening. Let's say the object of your affections is secretly a serial killer. Do you really not care what he or she has done as long as you are loved? Furthermore, just how much do you think a serial killer can love you?

As you read the lyrics of these songs, you may chuckle. The words seem romantic and harmless. Unfortunately, they perpetuate our expectation that relationships should make us feel good rather than make us grow. If we believe this myth, we can feel betrayed and persecuted when our relationships go through painful phases. We didn't, after all, sign up for growth when we picked our beloved. I frequently see clients who believe they must have picked the wrong partner because they don't feel good anymore. I remember one couple I worked with where the husband said in all seriousness, "A good wife never makes her husband feel bad."

When we get stuck searching for a "soul mate," it's because we're missing a connection with our own soul. When we don't have a connection with our insides, we're usually in pain and are often tempted to use relationships like drugs. The high of being in love is wonderful, but it can be as addicting as other substances, such as sugar, alcohol, or cocaine. The purpose of intimate relationships isn't to anesthetize our painful feelings but to open us to fully experiencing *all* our emotions. If we had realistic love songs, the lyrics might be: "I learn so much from being with you / I love the way we work a conflict through / It isn't easy knowing what to do / But the risks we take keep it feeling brand new!"

At work, we typically have beliefs that parallel romantic expectations. We may believe that professional relationships should make us feel confident, competent, and appreciated. Every week I get letters from readers of my syndicated column, "Interpersonal Edge," complaining about co-workers, bosses, and customers. When my readers are upset with people, they usually feel betrayed. Many readers believe others should change, not them. Social Sorcerers realize that if they wait for others to change, they'll live life feeling continually victimized. Remember that your power exists in changing yourself, not in waiting for others to transform.

Taking Back Your Power

Most of us like it when other people make us feel good, but a problem develops if we believe that good feelings are the primary purpose of being in a relationship, which should give us the opportunity to learn and to expand our soul's capacity for loving and living. When you believe that good feelings about yourself *must* come from others, you then place all the power in other people's hands.

It's normal to go through painful phases in relationships where you disagree more than you agree. The longer and more intimate your connection, the more painful and drawn out the conflict can be. If we stay in relationships only when we're comfortable, we don't learn to relate to ourselves or anyone else.

Pain in a relationship often signals the birth of new possibilities between ourselves and others. Think about the intense process of bringing a child into the world. If the mother and people around her decided that her discomfort meant that the process should stop, no one would create a family, and the human race would die out. Discomfort in your relationships can signal the birth of a new level of understanding. To forge a deeper connection, we need to breathe, talk about the pain, and commit to facilitating the process.

Some of the suffering we experience in relationships is unavoidable, and in fact, it can teach us how to make better choices. However, unnecessarily agonizing by putting yourself in positions where you're abused, walked on, or hurt isn't being enlightened—it's being foolish. Stories about Buddha's search for enlightenment say that he lived for a time with a group of ascetics who denied themselves all comforts. Buddha realized that suffering alone wasn't leading him to enlightenment, and he left (much to the dismay of the other ascetics).

We could avoid needless pain by paying attention to the Life Lab we're in, then changing our behavior. When we suffer unnecessarily, we're choosing to repeat mistakes without learning anything. Necessary suffering, on the other hand, is discomfort that encourages us to grow *up*, not just old.

Now that you know how to access the universal Help menu, change your emotional patterns through your relationships, and use discomfort to become wiser, the next chapter will show you how your soul uses difficult moments as a business plan for your enlightenment. No one looks forward to challenging situations, but you'll see how to *use* these occurrences in order to design your best possible future.

🌍 🌍 🌍

CHAPTER 17

A BUSINESS PLAN FOR THE SOUL

"The mind, once expanded to the dimensions of larger ideas, never returns to its original size."

— Oliver Wendell Holmes

The soul uses reactions to people as a business plan for one's development. Most of us have heard that if five people witness an accident, all five will have different versions of what happened, but we're usually less aware of how our own beliefs, assumptions, and attitudes can color our perception of people.

If you want an easy question to kick-start learning about yourself, contemplate whom you envy or detest. Your answers will reveal sides of you that are usually difficult for you to see. You can find your insides outside when you notice traits you admire or find repulsive in others.

Finding Your Insides Outside

For example, in a team-building group I conducted, there was a manager, Karl, who admired others for their public speaking. When the others heard this compliment, they were amazed because he was by far the most articulate speaker. Unfortunately, until Karl did the exercise in this chapter, he was unconscious of his gift of eloquence. When we're unaware of our strengths, we typically feel envy or admiration toward people we perceive as having those abilities, but we're not able to use these talents ourselves because we don't *see* them.

We don't just see positive parts of ourselves in others but negative qualities as well. When we're unaware of our less admirable traits, we may feel repulsion or hatred toward the person we believe possesses them. The danger in rejecting our weaknesses is that we may end up acting them out compulsively. People can excuse their actions by saying, "The devil made me do it!" In actuality, they're denying a part of themselves, not an invisible demon driving us to engage in destructive actions.

For example, it's often big news when religious leaders, who fight passionately against "sins of the flesh," end up in compromising positions. When you see people campaign fervently against an issue, you may now wonder . . . is their adversary within, without, or both? Most people who are effective at changing society first identify their inner foes before they try to combat that same problem in the outer world.

To use your relationships to identify strengths or weaknesses you may not see in yourself, pay attention to what you obsess about in others. There are many characteristics you may adore or despise in other people. If your reaction to a trait is lukewarm, your soul isn't emphasizing it for you. When your soul wants to get your attention, the behavior of the other person will generate an intensely negative or positive reaction. You'll also tend to see that quality in lots of other folks.

For example, my client Stephen was anxious and self-critical. Before working with me, he had been unaware of these traits. He only saw that his boss drove him crazy by frequently demanding better work. Stephen also talked about how his co-workers were never satisfied. When he wasn't irritated with how his colleagues made him feel, he resented his wife for what he perceived as constant criticism. Once he saw his own tendency to be self-critical, he stood up for himself more effectively and received better treatment from others.

Self-Esteem Is Not a Democracy

Eleanor Roosevelt once said, "No one can make you feel inferior without your consent." She meant that the negative remarks of others only get under our skin if they find an inner voice of agreement. If someone says your purple hair is ugly and you're *certain* you don't have purple hair, the remark won't affect you. You won't argue, try to demonstrate the truth, or obsess about it; you'll just walk away, shake your head, and wonder how long the other person has been color-blind.

If a comment made by someone else deeply bothers you, your struggle isn't limited to the person making the hurtful remark. You're also struggling with a voice inside you that agrees with the upsetting comment. Bucking up or ignoring your pain won't heal your vulnerability to these remarks. Often the statements that sting the most are the ones we heard frequently from our family members. Hearing criticisms we received in our childhood, such as "You're too sensitive" or "You're so selfish," can get us boiling mad. If we *only* fight with the person making the comment, we vanquish the outer foe without touching the inner critic. As author and meditation teacher Sally Kempton once observed, "It's hard to fight an enemy that has outposts in your head."

I have a client, Thomas, whose father was shaming, belittling, and critical. When Thomas first married, he got prickly every time his wife asked him where the milk was—since it was obvious to him that his wife thought he'd put the milk in the wrong place. He assumed that other people were constantly seeing his shortcomings and made a life out of combating his inner critic by trying to be perfect.

As Thomas made progress in therapy with me, he saw that he was tuned to "Self-Criticism 105.8," 24 hours a day. From our work together, he learned to turn the volume down on this station and decided being good enough was, well . . . good enough. He and his wife were even able to joke about things when he jumped to the assumption that she was criticizing him like his father. His wife would mischievously say, "Honey, do you miss your father?" Thomas would say, "No! No!" and stop *assuming* she was looking for his inadequacies. Thomas couldn't have stopped seeing criticism everywhere if he hadn't found the roots within himself first.

Toolkit for Becoming What You Envy

Bring to mind three people whose company you enjoy or whom you admire. It might be your sister, a friend, and a co-worker. What personality traits do you respect or envy in these people? You may appreciate your sister because she stands up for what she believes, your friend because she's smart and outspoken, and a co-worker because he's a risk taker.

Is the trait you admire or envy in these three people one you don't see in yourself but wish you had? Write down that trait.

Now go to the nearest mirror, look into your eyes, and say: "I [your name], have the quality of [insert the trait you just identified]."

Now make a list of all the things you'd try if you *owned* this trait.

I heard someone say a long time ago that it's important to cultivate graciousness around people who intimidate us. If we can be gracious when we're jealous or in awe of someone, we get to associate with those who remind us of our own amazing potential. If we're merely consumed by jealousy, we lose the option to be inspired by people who could help us design a better business plan for our lives.

An Example of Becoming What You Envy

Darrick admired his dad, brother, and best friend for their risk taking and success in business. He'd always wanted to start his own law firm, but saw himself as too timid and unimaginative to put out his own shingle. When Darrick used this tool, he remembered how he convinced his university to grant him a scholarship to law school, how quickly he'd accumulated loyal clients as a new attorney, and the risk he recently took to leave a large firm and work for a smaller company that he admired. Once Darrick realized the qualities of bravery and competency he admired in his "heroes" were also part of him, he found the courage to start his own firm. Darrick's business became profitable within two years, but he believes that the *best* reward is the emotional paycheck he gets from running his own business.

Toolkit for Avoiding What You Hate

This exercise identifies ways in which your current relationships mirror weaknesses in yourself.

Think of three people who drive you crazy or annoy you. For instance, you may detest your father, your boss, and your sister's boyfriend.

What personality traits do you dislike in these people? You may feel antagonism toward your father because he didn't stand up for you, your boss because he lets everyone treat him like a doormat, and your sister's boyfriend because he's verbally abusive.

How are these qualities similar to your own personality traits? You may, for instance, struggle to protect yourself and stand your ground in relationships.

These other people will usually remind us of our own weakness. When we feel contempt for them, we also feel contempt for the part of us that's similar to them. If we get stuck constantly complaining about these people, we miss two opportunities:

1. We don't notice our struggle with this issue.

2. By judging this behavior, we make it harder to accept our own challenges in this area. Understanding and criticism can't occupy the same internal space. It's tough to understand ourselves if we're *judging* our behavior, and our behavior won't change unless we *understand* it first.

An Example of Avoiding What You Hate

Beth felt contempt for her co-worker, her neighbor, and her sister because they were overweight. She saw them as weak, undisciplined, and out of control. When Beth used this toolkit, she saw that although she didn't overeat, she was concerned about her drinking and her poor choices in guys. Previously she'd simply chalked up her hangovers from drinking and her bad love affairs to her need for more discipline. She started to see that she drank heavily and wasn't discriminating in her choice of male companions because she was terribly lonely. Beth also saw that criticizing herself for being weak wasn't helping her change. She finally admitted she needed help, joined Alcoholics Anonymous, and made several new girlfriends. As she accepted her own challenge, she realized that she had newfound compassion for the emotional pain of others whom she had formerly despised for being weak or out of control.

Many religions emphasize that refraining from judging others is the "high and holy thing to do." These spiritual teachings imply that our ability to avoid judging people on planet Earth will produce future heavenly benefits for us. However, most of us are more motivated by immediate self-interest than what will earn us future points in heaven. We may struggle to be "good," but judging other people simply gives us a profound feeling of relief.

When we complain about others, we actually vent our frustrations about our own weaknesses. Unfortunately, we usually don't realize that we're talking about ourselves. The traditional religious advice has told us *what* to do for centuries, but not *how* to achieve the goal or *why* it will help us. If we can use our judgments about others to learn about ourselves, we can liberate ourselves from habits that limit us right now. You don't have to wait until you die to experience the rewards. This doesn't mean that you can't huff and puff about how terrible someone is acting. It means that after you get done huffing and puffing, take a good look in the mirror.

What Your Shadow Knows

When you find your insides outside, you'll see how other people can show you your strengths and weaknesses. Now we'll go further into inner space and find out how you may be hiding entire inner personalities from yourself.

Swiss psychologist Carl Jung believed that your Spirit guides your life and relationships. He believed people had two selves: the self with a small "s" who pays bills and manages survival and the Self with a capital "S" who is aligned with the soul and guides us to our optimal potential.

Jung also thought that people went beyond hiding simple emotional reactions such as jealousy or hatred from themselves. He believed that people could hide entire personalities in what he called the "shadow self." The inner parts of ourselves that are most threatening, powerful, and foreign to the rest of our personality can be found in our *shadow*. Without therapy or emotional work of some kind, we're usually completely unaware of what we've hidden away. However, relationships give us great opportunities to see our shadow. When it's activated, our reactions will seem foreign or out of proportion to the trigger event. Our reactions or fascination for our shadow self may even seem crazy or out of control.

For instance, the shadow personality of a priest might become fascinated with pornography. The shadow personality of a very rational executive can cause him to fall hopelessly in love with an extremely emotional woman. The shadow personality of a timid employee might draw him to support the actions of an aggressive, abusive boss.

Our shadow self tries to keep us emotionally balanced. We're drawn irrationally and powerfully toward what we can't see inside ourselves. We then have the opportunity to claim and integrate those qualities—if we're paying attention. Our Self with a big "S" can use our relationships to create a spiritual challenge to *know* and *accept* all parts of ourselves.

My Shadow Made Me Do It?

Many spiritual practices have taught that "God is love." These same spiritual traditions usually tell us that we should love ourselves and love each other. Since most of us are fairly imperfect, this ambitious goal can seem like a cosmic joke. On a billboard in Seattle a few years back, there was a huge picture of Martin Luther King, Jr. The billboard said: "Love is not the answer, it's the assignment." If we use relationships as a spiritual path, we actually apprentice ourselves in a practical way every day to love. Loving the shadow parts of ourselves means that we accept all our feelings and impulses.

Accepting or loving our shadow means no longer acting out the feelings within it without thinking. For instance, you may be so mad that you could kill someone. If you can fully experience this intense anger internally, you'll have more choice over what you do externally. You improve your chances of expressing your rage in conversation, not homicide. The parts of your shadow that remain in the dark will continue to manipulate your behavior, and you'll feel helpless. People who suffer daily from addictive or compulsive behavior are often struggling with their shadow.

I once knew a man named David who was a Pentecostal Christian. Consciously David wanted to be kind, spiritually mature, a good father, and a loving husband. Unfortunately, David had a very well-hidden shadow he wouldn't accept. He confessed to me at one point that his life was spinning out of control and felt like a charade. He'd been going to prostitutes throughout his marriage, seeking anonymous bisexual partners, and slipping into alcoholism. His behavior was so foreign and against David's core beliefs that he became suicidal. David was so sure he was bad that he never did wrestle with the healthy emotional needs underneath his self-destructive behavior. If he'd understood these parts of himself, he might have opened up new levels of intimacy with himself and others.

I lost track of him for about a year, and when we reconnected, he was divorced, alone, alienated from his kids, had lost his business, and his health was failing as well. As David's case shows, our soul always gives us a choice: Either face our shadow or be destroyed by it.

The shadow can also exert an irrational, powerful draw over our choice of partners. Amelia, a client who was sweet and nice, fell in love with Daniel, who was angry and often alienated people. She consciously valued being cooperative, helpful, and reasonable. He was rude, pushy, and nasty—a perfect balance to my client's overemphasis on niceness.

Amelia and her boyfriend also fought a great deal, which helped teach her about anger. Amelia's undeveloped shadow personality drew her to this boyfriend. As she owned her hidden self, she accepted her anger and learned to say no to people. Daniel became less fascinating to her, and Amelia was able to easily leave the abusive relationship.

Trying to see our shadow is similar to sitting in a car and straining to see the blind spot. Jung believed that the way to see this blind area was to use our irrational, intense reactions to other people as a mirror. Shadow qualities in ourselves always provoke extremely positive or negative responses when we see them in others. If you righteously hate people who are liars, there may be a way in which you don't always tell the truth. If you don't respect liars, but you don't have strong feelings toward them, lying is unlikely to be part of your hidden self. Your shadow may also appear in your dreams if you recall a character, the same gender as you, who has either wonderful or terrible qualities.

Toolkit for Your Shadow

Think of traits you find admirable in others. You don't even need to know these people. You can bring to mind movie stars, writers, athletes, or political figures. Include the qualities of those you've fallen madly in love with and thought you couldn't live without. What is it about these people you've been powerfully drawn toward?

Are there positive shadow qualities you'd like to develop in yourself? Write them down. For instance, my friend Carol fell deeply in love with Joel, who was passionate and playful. There were many problems in the relationship, as Joel was unfaithful, abusive, and irresponsible, but Carol couldn't leave him. She was a highly disciplined, successful workaholic, but she eventually understood that Joel reflected her playful, passionate shadow self. As she was able to be passionate and play more, Carol became less mesmerized with Joel, left him, and picked a kind-hearted boyfriend.

What qualities do you hate vehemently in others? Again, this may be people you don't know: actors on a television series, media personalities, or even a book character. You may break out in hives around people who exhibit know-it-all, arrogant behavior. You may dislike this behavior so much that you turn off the television when an egotistical actor comes on. Write these traits down as well.

How are these qualities similar to ones you have (even if less intense)?

Now look at the positive and negative shadow qualities you've identified. Can you think of ways in which you also possess these traits?

If you hate arrogance, you may notice that when you're nervous, you act like you know what you're doing rather than admit uncertainty. You may also find you get quiet and aloof when you're anxious. When you identify shadow qualities in yourself, you'll understand other people better. You'll realize that they often do things because they have the same emotional vulnerability you do. For example, in the future, if you meet someone who acts arrogant, you might realize that they could just be anxious. You'll also find it easier to contain your own feelings, talk about your insecurities, get support, and not feel that you have to be the master of every situation.

When you first think about the negative-shadow question, don't be surprised if you get annoyed or insist that you don't have any of *those* qualities. Our negative shadow is full of painful emotions, and most of us are uncomfortable looking into that dark cave of feelings. In addition, don't be surprised if when you think about the positive-shadow question, you insist that little old you certainly couldn't have any of those amazing qualities. Shadow characteristics are outside of normal consciousness and are hard to bring into awareness—that's why they're called your shadow.

An Example of Your Shadow

Martin tended to choose women who were stunningly beautiful, aloof, and self-centered. He was drawn to them like a moth to a flame, and the aftermath of most of his affairs left him feeling burned. When Martin first tried this toolkit, he insisted that he didn't have any of the qualities of the women he chose. However, after much reflection, he realized that he was scared of falling really in love and getting hurt. He had a wall around him that kept him safe but kept other people out—thus, he picked women who wouldn't let him get close. As Martin worked with this tool, he chose to date a woman, Donna, who wasn't his usual type—she was warm, affectionate, and wanted to be married. Instead of being controlled by his shadow and running the other way, Martin let his guard down and ended up married very contentedly to Donna.

When you know your shadow, it's less likely to take over and run your life by influencing you to behave impulsively. Carl Jung believed that the threat of nuclear war was an example of our collective shadow putting the survival of our entire world at risk. He believed that we wouldn't survive as a species, unless we individually owned our shadows.

There's a story often told about a drunk who's looking for his keys underneath a lamppost. A kind police officer comes along and offers to help find the lost keys. As both the officer and inebriated man search under the lamppost, the officer finally asks, "Where *exactly* were your keys lost?" The man points to a dark alley. The officer then scratches his head and asks the man, "Why are we looking for the keys under this lamppost if you lost the keys in the alley?" The drunk says simply, "The light's better here."

Like this inebriated man, we often search for the keys to life's challenges by seeking solutions in the easiest places to look. Unfortunately, these locations don't have the answers we need to give us the lives we want. Therefore, in the next chapter, I'll be giving you a map for venturing off popular well-lit roads onto the darker, less-traveled paths where the most powerful secrets of life await you.

CHAPTER 18

WAKING UP

*"Do not follow where the path may lead.
Go instead where there is no path and leave a trail."*
— Ralph Waldo Emerson

Louise, a client who'd been practicing Social Sorcery, recently came to my office and said with astonishment, "I'm just realizing that most people don't think—they're on automatic! I realize I'm thinking about even *little* choices. Like today, I went to get a burrito. I always get the regular burrito. I was thinking about trying to lower my carbs as I waited in line and realized I *could* get a smaller size and it would still taste as good. Now I know this doesn't sound like a big deal, but normally I would have just sleepwalked through the line. I'm so excited to be able to see *all* of my choices."

Making Your Own Map

Louise is right, most people *are* sleepwalking—*you,* however, are waking up. You're more aware that small decisions about burritos won't make or break your life, but your ability to see all of your options will. Albert Einstein commented on the necessity of lifting our level of consciousness when he said, "The significant problems we face today can't be solved at the same level of thinking we were at when we created them."

As you use Social Sorcery, your life will improve and you'll feel more and more extraordinary. However, when you start to change your habits, you may look slightly different to some folks. People around you think they know you and can predict your behavior, so they don't expect you to suddenly leave the well-traveled paths that make up *their* maps of the "known world."

On ancient mariners' maps, adventurous sailors were warned away from too much exploration with the reminder that at the edge of the familiar world, "There be dragons." Now I've always thought seeking out dragons would be a good reason to leave the ordinary world behind. After all, dragons were supposed to guard great magic, and if you tamed one—you *might* just get to fly.

If a few people get nervous as you sail off the edge of *their* known maps, you can let them in on the secret that most of the really good stuff in life is off the beaten path.

Ending the Blame Drain

Changing the ingrained patterns we learned from our original family is the "grand prix" of spiritual challenge in life. In our families, we got used to certain ways of relating. Typically, over time, we internalized these patterns by treating ourselves the way our family treated us. We also treat others as we were treated and expect other people to act in ways our relatives acted. Our family's automatic interactions work fine in areas where we related effectively, but we get in all sorts of trouble in areas where our family related poorly.

Let's say that your father was emotionally distant and a perfectionist. At work, when your boss asks you to pay closer attention to details, you may feel incensed. You might fume inwardly about how nothing you do is ever good enough. In your personal relationships, you may be hypersensitive to dissatisfaction from your partner. If your partner complains, you might explode because you feel that this means he or she doesn't love you.

When we believe that other people are treating us like our family did, something called "projection" may be occurring. When we're projecting, it's as if we have a movie projector showing old family movies on top of someone's face in our current life. Sometimes there's truth to our projection. For example, if you actually have a controlling boss and you were raised by a controlling mother, you aren't just projecting domineering qualities onto your boss. However, due to your mother's behavior, it's more likely that you'll be upset by your boss's controlling manner than other folks. When people make a request for change or some other innocent remark, you'll have a tendency to perceive it as a command and overreact. If a co-worker says, "Have a good weekend," you might think, *Don't tell me what kind of weekend to have!*

We often assume that our irritated reactions are caused by other people's intentions. We can get huffy without understanding the reasons for our feelings. It's like having an old football injury that aches when it rains. However, with this type of injury, we know that it isn't the *fault* of the rain because we remember the original wound. With emotional damage, we usually don't connect our current pain to the initial injuries in childhood. Thus, we blame whoever is standing in front of us when we're upset. Our logic can work like this: "If I'm hurting, then the person I'm dealing with must be up to no good." We usually don't stop and ask other people what they intended; we simply assume negative motives.

We can also project positive family history onto others; for example, when we fall in love, we may project all the positive patterns of our family onto our newly beloved. As time goes on, our affirmative projections wear thin. We then find out if our partner *really* possesses these qualities. At this point, we often panic because we desperately want our partner to possess all of these wonderful traits. As our ideal projected partner fades and the real person emerges, the tough work of a relationship begins.

Unfortunately, we often divorce or split up when this happens because we believe that if we were really in love, our *projection* would last forever. We think our idealistic perceptions were accurate. Our partner *really* was perfect, but he or she has changed. We fail to see that it's merely our perception that has changed. We're now seeing who our partner actually was all along.

When I'm working with a married couple and their projections are fading, they usually feel betrayed and furious. I encourage them by telling them that they *now* have the opportunity to stop dating and learn to be married. We only have a chance to deeply get to know our spouse when we stop seeing them through the rosy glasses of being infatuated or "in love." When our projections fade, the real person we married emerges from beneath our family home movie. If we don't understand what has happened, we can feel unbearably misled, and separate from our former sweetheart with great bitterness. If we realize that the projection was an illusion all along and let go of our fantasies about perfect love, then we can be happily married.

Anytime you begin a new relationship at work, make a new friend, or start a new love affair, you'll be prone to idealizing your situation. If you anticipate that the initial glow will wear off, you'll see the potential problems earlier, be less upset by the predictable conflicts, and understand that perpetual paradise only exists in fairy tales.

Toolkit for Ending the Blame Drain

The following questions will help you explore what particular patterns of projection might exist in your current relationships:

1. Write down some positive, happy memories you have of your family as a child. You might remember enjoying long conversations when your mother would teach you about the world. Maybe your father was playful or silly, and he gave you pony rides on his back in the yard. Your recollections may include memories of your brothers, sisters, or friends playing baseball with you on warm summer evenings.

2. How are these memories similar to qualities you look for in your relationships now (personal and professional)? For example, if you remember having wonderful intellectual conversations with your mother, do you project all sorts of positive qualities onto people who seem intellectual? If your dad was playful, do you immediately feel comfortable with people who are humorous and physically affectionate? If you loved those baseball moments, you may still be drawn to people in situations where you can be part of a team and experience camaraderie.

3. What kinds of painful memories do you have of relating to your family as a child? Perhaps your sister was jealous, competitive, and always tried to get you into trouble. Your father may have worked so much that he was never around when you needed him. Perhaps you didn't have any siblings and felt isolated from other kids.

4. How are these memories similar to experiences you avoid or find difficult as an adult? For example, if your sister was always your rival, you may find that it's tough to work cooperatively or trust women at work. If you felt you could never get your father's attention or approval, do you avoid situations where you might feel inadequate or there's a possibility of failure? If you felt isolated as an only child, do you find group work difficult and believe that you'll end up not being included?

When you identify your old family movies, you can stop playing reruns of *A Nightmare on <u>Your</u> Street* as you go through life. If you understand the ways that your family history colored your current perceptions, you can live your life in the present and not be trapped by your past. Through awareness of your projection patterns, you'll find that it's never too late to have a happy childhood—as long as the wounded child in you doesn't keep running the show.

An Example of Ending the Blame Drain

Stewart fell in love with Maggie immediately. She was fiery, smart, and athletic—just like his mom. But after a whirlwind romance and wedding, he began to avoid going home at night to his new bride. He now found her argumentative, exhausting, and demanding. When Stewart used this tool, he realized that he'd idealized Maggie and had expected her to treat him like a son, not a husband. He realized that her fiery nature and intelligence were stimulating *and* tiring. He started to enjoy her energy again, stopped expecting her to be his mom, and talked with her about needing breaks when he became overwhelmed.

How to Gain from the Pain

My client Susanna is fond of saying, "When I'm supposed to learn a life lesson, the whole universe lines up to kick me in the rear." Susannah is observing that when our soul conspires to teach us an interpersonal lesson, everything and everyone seems in on a "plot" to make us grow up in a way we've been avoiding. I find that the greater our resistance to change, the bigger the bat that hits us upside the head.

When events conspire to get you to make a change, you're the much-loved recipient of a "cosmic wake-up call." Like a real wake-up call, it's natural to hit the snooze button several times. The more uncomfortable our issue, the more times we hit the button.

Eventually, we're presented with a dilemma regarding a difficult situation. Do we want to continue to believe in an unfair universe that's being mean to us, or do we want to rouse ourselves and make meaning out of painful events? Even truly horrible situations can be endured if something significant can be derived from them. Neurologist and psychiatrist Viktor Frankl, when imprisoned in a Nazi concentration camp, developed a theory of psychology based on the idea that unless people find meaning, they have no reason to live. He noted that the people who survived the concentration camps appeared to make meaning out of what they were going through and hold tightly to what they valued. According to Frankl, many individuals who wasted away seemed to give up a search for meaning early on.

The universe provides us with an infinitely patient educational program. We never have to learn anything *now,* but the intensity of the lesson does keep increasing. I remember a man, Bennet, who was an expert at avoiding short-term emotional pain. He continually mortgaged his future to avoid present discomfort. At every life-choice point, he would avoid growing or changing. He took drugs, went bankrupt, lost his business, lost his family, went from one empty relationship to the next, and alienated the people who loved him. He continued to grow more depressed, empty, and unhappy. Up until the time I lost track of Bennet, the universe kept sending him bigger and badder wake-up calls, but he stubbornly refused to change.

If we keep operating like Bennet, we'll need to find stronger ways of numbing ourselves to pain each time a bigger bat hits us. Our life then becomes a series of challenges about how *much* suffering we can endure and how to continue to try to look like we're okay. We may drink, become workaholics, have affairs, overspend, obsessively play video games, or watch mind-numbing amounts of television—anything to avoid facing ourselves.

If we're willing, eventually we shut off the white noise distracting us from ourselves. We switch off the television, stop trying to find the perfect partner, and put down the martini. We sit quietly with our thoughts, emotions, and unfulfilled dreams. We then find that we *can* stand the feelings, they don't kill us, and they do make us wiser. As we get to know ourselves, we may learn that many of the things we've avoided our whole life represented a feeling or a part of ourselves we didn't think we could tolerate.

Many of these blocks about emotions or thoughts were developed when we were little kids, but they're still controlling us.

You may have had an angry parent who yelled and hit. If so, you may grow up to be an adult who's terrified of anger both in yourself and in others. Anytime someone's angry, you may feel like a defenseless child dealing with a big, scary parent. As an adult, you may not see how to protect yourself even though the resources to do so are now available. You may also be afraid of your own anger because you believe that you might turn into an angry monster—just like your parent.

Toolkit for How to Gain from the Pain

If you respond to your life challenges as a spiritual wake-up call, you can see your life as an intelligently unfolding curriculum uniquely constructed for your enrichment. Use the following exercises to help identify the patterns your soul has been highlighting for you to change:

1. What "recurrent themes" do you notice in your relationships? A recurrent theme is one you've experienced in a variety of relationships. For instance, in your career, you may always end up working for people who take advantage of you. You may pick relationships where your romantic partners meet their needs at your expense. If you look at your friends, you may notice that they enjoy your support but are rather self-absorbed. The theme here would be that you tend to tolerate or choose people who are self-centered.

2. In what other relationships have you experienced similar problems? How did you react or feel? You may remember that you've often felt as if people are selfish or don't like to be around you if it's the least bit inconvenient. You may remember friendships when you were a child or relationships with teachers. Be sure to think about your early relationships with your family. For example, did your mom expect you to always be an obedient, good child? Did your dad go into a rage if you disagreed with him or asked him for anything? If you became accustomed to self-centeredness in your family, you may find this treatment "normal" and have trouble confronting people who have no empathy for the needs of others.

3. Has the pattern you've identified changed over time (gotten more or less intense or happens more or less frequently)? How has it changed? If you've put up with narcissistic people, are you starting to select people who are more empathetic and better at reciprocation? For instance, your current boss may be arrogant but actually listens to your ideas and is helping mentor you. Over time most of us get smarter about how we handle others, but we often don't notice our progress. If you can *see* the ways you've *already* improved your decision making, you'll more easily build on your past successes, and be better able to fix problems in your current relationships before they start.

When you've finished these exercises, talk about them with a friend. Or if you prefer, write them down in a journal. When you do so, contemplate how you can react differently to the people who are difficult for you. Think about how you typically handle the feelings triggered by these tough relationships, and entertain options you wouldn't usually consider.

An Example of How to Gain from the Pain

Jeanette noticed that she often picked people to work with and befriend who were intellectual and critical. She was "killing" herself at work to get her boss's approval, and she remembered that her dad always focused on *her* mistakes and *his* superiority. When Jeanette used this tool, she decided that she was tired of feeling like she always had to prove she was smart. She also realized that people who treated her like she was dumb were abusive and wouldn't change even if she did come off as more brilliant. Even if Jeanette felt intimidated when she was around smart, critical people, she expressed her ideas. If someone criticized her thinking, she said, "I can see that we view this differently," and continued to voice her opinions. She started going home at 5 P.M., refused to work weekends, and found the time to have a boyfriend for the first time in years. Jeanette realized that the only person whose approval she couldn't live without was her own—everyone else's good opinion was optional.

Congratulations! You've just finished the last toolkit you'll need to master your Social Sorcery skills. And now, as an official Social Sorcerer, you've aligned yourself with truth and love. As you put your new skills into practice, you'll begin to experience an amazing freedom to positively change yourself and your world. The rest of this chapter will show you how to combine all the magic you've learned to turn your dreams into reality.

The Zen of Relationships

As you master these techniques, they'll reward you with increased spiritual development and effectiveness in the world. Most of us don't have the time to retreat to a remote monastery to increase our consciousness. Now you won't have to leave your ordinary life to develop your spirituality because your Social Sorcery toolkits will allow you to use your everyday relationships (both business and personal) as an "active spiritual meditation."

The tools you've learned will also provide you with many of the same benefits as years of meditation (without retreating from your normal life). You'll find yourself increasingly in a state of mindfulness (being aware of the present moment). When your thoughts were agitated in the past, you might have felt as if you were in the middle of a pond, swimming frantically and stirring up the muddy water. But now, as you use your toolkits, you'll be able to calm your thoughts, the mud will settle to the bottom, and you'll have the clarity to know what to do and say to get what you need. You'll increasingly find a calm center inside of you, like the eye of a hurricane, even though the storms of life continue to swirl around you.

When you have the Interpersonal Edge, you'll discover delicious new options in your life. You'll be manipulated less often because you'll have better control of your reactions. Even if you can't *stop* your reactions, you'll be capable of noticing your feelings. Instead of being paralyzed by your emotions or reacting automatically, you'll then choose the behavior that will work best in your situation.

As a Social Sorcerer, you'll improve your relationships with other people and with the one person you can never escape from—yourself. As you actively "meditate" on whatever is occurring in your relationships you'll find that you judge others and yourself less. You'll also find that you're kinder with yourself as you become liberated from your unquestioned assumptions, automatic emotional reactions, and painful family patterns.

Just like a rocket uses the most energy escaping the gravitational pull of the earth, you'll likely find that the toughest part of Social Sorcery is the beginning of your learning curve. But, as you soar free of your former limitations, you'll be rewarded with creative solutions to your most persistent problems and discover an inner peace that is building inside of you.

That's not to say that you won't have negative thoughts and emotions sometimes, but you'll be able to choose the most powerful course of action anyway. It's similar to shopping at the grocery store that has soft Muzak playing. You don't stop buying your produce and cry whenever you hear a sad song. You notice the song, feel sentimental, and buy your broccoli—because that's why you came to the store. With the Interpersonal Edge, your feelings and thoughts will become more like the quiet background Muzak, controlling your reactions less.

You'll discover a tranquility and detachment because you won't be desperately clinging to one preconceived outcome. And the coolest part is that you'll be able to achieve these results while at your kid's soccer game, your performance evaluation at work, or disagreeing with your significant other. You'll even be able to notice once-in-a-lifetime opportunities coming your way because you'll be more flexible and open-minded when the universe changes plans on you.

As I finish walking this part of your journey with you, I want to congratulate you for your devotion to yourself, your commitment to your dreams, and your courage. Although I haven't met you yet, I admire your willingness to look at yourself and find your new wings.

There's a story often told about a man who upon dying meets a guide and asks about heaven and hell. "I will show you hell," says the guide. And they go into a room with a delicious pot of soup in the middle. Around the pot sit people who are miserable and starving because they're holding spoons with handles longer than their arms, and it's impossible to get any soup into their mouths. "Now I will show you heaven," says the guide. They go into an identical room with a similar pot and people with the same spoons. But these folks are all well nourished, chatting amiably, and very happy. At first the man is confused until the guide explains, "It's simple. You see, they've learned to use the spoons to feed each other."

With the Interpersonal Edge, you'll live your daily life with the practical skills you need to handle people compassionately and effectively, whether it's your rebellious kids, cranky spouse, or a backstabbing co-worker. And the best part is that you don't have to change your circumstances. No matter what your current challenges are, your new tools will allow you to nourish your professional and personal relationships to create your own heaven on earth.

AFTERWORD

Throughout this book you've been working out in an "interpersonal gym," building emotional muscle through the toolkits. Just as you do when getting physically fit, you've also been learning a new *language*. As you get buff at the gym, you learn terms such as *Pilates* or *resting heart rate*. As you've developed the Interpersonal Edge, you've learned terms such as *"I" language, mystical abnormality, paraphrasing,* and *Tele-visioning*.

In each chapter, you've developed your fluency in the language of Social Sorcery and will now be able to speak to anyone, anywhere, at any time, in ways that optimize your chances of getting what you want. You now have the flexibility to speak the "interpersonal" dialect of the person you're with, or the place where you happen to be. Your new language will help you command respect in the workplace, get cooperation from your unruly kids, and create intimacy with your beloved without needing to change who you are.

As your life takes off, you'll notice an unexpected outcome—people around you will also benefit when you take better care of yourself. You won't just be improving your own life; you'll also be making a difference in the lives of everyone you touch.

When you get fit, it's a thrill to put on clothes that show off your results. When you have the Interpersonal Edge, it's truly exciting to step out into the world and realize that you're in the driver's seat. So the next time your boss tries to take advantage of you or your kids are whining or your in-laws are coming to visit—you won't feel powerless because you can go straight to a reliable toolkit. You'll be surprised how much stronger, smarter, and more effective you are at work and at home. The emotional muscles you've built by using your new tools will reveal the power, wisdom, and serenity that have been lying dormant within you.

Most of us love stories about heroes and heroines who overcome daunting trials to find the magic that was within them all along. I wrote this book to remind you that *you* are that hero or heroine. No matter what your situation, there are astonishing forces within you that are equal to any challenge.

You're already in the right place, with the right people, and doing what you need to do. *Listen* to your inner self, *fight* for yourself, and *trust* your new Interpersonal Edge to create a life you absolutely love!

ACKNOWLEDGMENTS

I believe passionately in the power and preciousness of gratitude. I feel profoundly fortunate to have had the people, circumstances, and opportunities that support my work in the world. This book was influenced and helped by more people than I can briefly list. I'm enormously thankful to the following people for supporting me and this book:

Ariana, who's an incredible daughter and teacher (and likes the idea that she's now a "famous baby" because her stories are in the book). My husband, Bruce, who's my best friend, amazing supporter, and has shown me what real loves looks like. Judy Long-Severance, my best friend, soul sister, wise advisor, and so much more that she's a book in herself. Larry Severance, who's the brother I never had. My colleagues and friends Kathleen Tyrrell, Steven Mitchell, and Mark Yamada, who have supported this book and me by being courageous companions on the path of original experience.

I'm grateful to my sisters, Jodie and Lisa, for being childhood playmates, loving me, and "seeing" me when we were little. I appreciate my mother and father for lighting the fire in me to do this work and showing me why it was important. Thanks to my stepdad, Jon, because you have a big heart and take good care of my mother. And to my stepdad, Cam, thanks for loving me, listening to me, and staying connected. For my extended family, Sharon and Bob Rudd, their children, and the Poussier clan, you've shown me what a healthy family looks like and have embraced my family with loving arms.

I've had incredible teachers in my life who include: Peter Geiler and my colleagues at the Institute for Movement Therapy; Gene

Kidder, who told me there was always a career for a person brave enough to explore the path of original experience and knew who I was before I did; Harriet Lerner, for being an inspiration, generous mentor, and model of what integrity, truth, and courage look like in the world.

To the staff and students in the work- and personal-development programs at Bellevue Community College: The staff and administrators, especially, are a model for soulful communication in the workplace and a heck of a lot of fun to work with.

Many thanks as well to present and former colleagues at *The Seattle Times:* Debbie Van Tassel, former *Seattle Times* business editor, now assistant managing editor at the *Cleveland Plain Dealer.* Debbie gave my "Dear Abby in the workplace" column a chance and believed in me as a writer. Thanks to Carol Pucci, my talented, patient first editor at *The Times,* who taught me how to write for a newspaper. Becky Bisbee, *The Seattle Times* business editor, a highly competent manager, and a model for love in action. Bill Kossen, *The Seattle Times* jobs editor, and every writer's dream editor. He went beyond changing my semicolons and made me think about writing with humor, clarity, and compassion. You have experienced Mr. Bill's magical touch in my writing throughout this book. Frank Blethen, publisher and CEO of *The Times;* and David Boardman, managing editor, for hiring and supporting such talented people.

Doug Page at Tribune Media, because from the first time I talked to him, I knew that I only wanted his company to syndicate my column. He's a solid, good-hearted, and talented sales manager. All of the people at Tribune Media that I've met have impressed me with their professionalism, aliveness, and effectiveness.

To Monique Mallory, my publicist, who is an all-round cool person with great intuition. This book wouldn't have ended up with the right publisher without you.

To Jo-Lynne Worley and Joanie Shoemaker, my agents, for believing in my work and being who you are. I am continually delighted to be working with you.

To Reid Tracy and the folks at Hay House for committing to this book. Out of all the publishing houses, Hay House was my first choice. To Jill Kramer, Shannon Littrell, and Jessica Vermooten, my editors at Hay House, for smoothing out my writing and making sure the manuscript was error free.

To Cliff Carle, my freelance editor, thank you for your personal engagement, honesty, and thoughtful responses to the material. Your practical suggestions made this book clearer, easier to read, and much more helpful to the reader.

To my corporate and private-therapy clients, you're my inspiration and my teachers, and you give me hope for the human race. Your courage, tenacity, and openness allow me to see the best of what people can become.

To the readers of my column "Interpersonal Edge," you challenged me to write this book so that you could have the tools behind the column. Thank you for your letters, stories, and questions.

To all the people who eagerly read and gave feedback on early drafts of the book (you know who you are).

I stand on the shoulders of so many wise authors, teachers, and explorers of inner space that I can't list them all. The short list includes: John Bradshaw, Joseph Campbell, Carl Jung, Alice Miller, Deepak Chopra, Gail Sheehy, Deborah Tannen, Gay Hendricks, Kathlyn Hendricks, Harville Hendrix, Arnold Mindell, John Gray, Stephen Gilligan, Linda Schierse Leonard, Wayne Dyer, Louise Hay, Roger Fisher, and William Ury.

I'm also grateful to my adversaries in life, for my struggles with you have taught me much about patience, courage, and creativity.

Last, and most completely, I'm grateful to the Spirit that infuses everything; and the help, affection, and wisdom from which my life springs. None of what I have done would be possible without such support.

ABOUT THE AUTHOR

Daneen Skube, Ph.D., the director of Interpersonal Edge, has worked in the field of business consulting, counseling, and speaking for more than 27 years. Her company specializes in helping individuals and companies achieve peak performance through strategic communication skills.

Dr. Skube's lively and highly entertaining training and speaking engagements have helped Fortune 500 companies, health-care organizations, government agencies, and family and small businesses improve productivity and create harmony in the workplace. Her executive coaching and therapy practice has helped hundreds of individuals identify and achieve their dreams. Dr. Skube's column, "Interpersonal Edge," internationally syndicated through Tribune Media Services, has been assisting readers with workplace- and people-related issues for over a decade. She's the "Workplace Guru" for Q13 (FOX channel's Monday-morning news in Seattle), and a member of the Society of American Business Editors and Writers.

Dr. Skube lives with her husband, daughter, and two cats in the foothills of the Cascade Mountains in Issaquah, Washington. For more information or to receive her free newsletter, please visit: **www.interpersonaledge.com**.

NOTES

NOTES

NOTES

NOTES

NOTES

NOTES